FROM
CORRECTIONS
TO CAREERS

Today's Foodservice Workforce

KIM NUGENT, Ed.D.

Publisher: JETLAUNCH

Paperback ISBN: 978-1-960995-89-6
eBook ISBN: 978-1-960995-90-2

Contact Kim Nugent, Ed.D at:
Email: nugent1234@gmail.com or Kim@drnugentspeaks.com
Website: www.drnugentspeaks.com

Credits:
Cover Designs, Interior Layout & Design: Jetlaunch Publishing

TESTIMONIALS

Dr. Nugent has identified—and now filled—a critical gap in reducing recidivism while also providing relief to the ongoing labor shortage in the food service industry. This includes a sound approach to identifying careers in the food service industry for previously incarcerated women and men, one that provides guidance on recruiting, retaining, and developing candidates for careers in food service for hospitality managers. This book is long overdue and represents a solid contribution to society.

Dennis Reynolds, Ph.D.
Dean of the College and Barron Hilton Distinguished Chair
University of Houston Conrad N. Hilton College of
Global Hospitality Leadership
der@uh.edu

I have 25 years of prior security experience at a maximum-security state penitentiary. I have worked with all classes of offenders; I have always had an open mind to accept people for what they are now and not what they were then. Being here in this smaller facility I have had the opportunity to work with these offenders in a closer environment.

It has been a pleasure to interview the mentees and find out a small amount about them. The biggest percentage is looking for a purpose of being accepted, needed, and a part of something. The mentorship program allows them to come out for group sessions and enjoy being in the presence of others. These guys get the chance to express themselves and are taken to a higher level than they ever expected. The mentees can accompany the mentors into the kitchen to participate in hands-on training. Sometimes, we share special meals with them. I sometimes sit in on their open discussion sessions. During the discussions, I hear a lot of (I did not know dealing with food was this exciting) and when they get the chance to do on hands the smiles on their faces say it all. I have seen a change in some of their attitudes for the better.

Martha P.
Correctional Facility Foodservice Director

I cannot overstate the impact of both mentorship programs, but more specifically, Today's Food Service Workforce. At its inception here at Wilkinson County Correctional Facility, designed to provide targeted training and job readiness skills while enhancing employability, the program tapped into the imaginations of the men here. It allowed them to think about the food service industry not only from a societal perspective but also from a corrections perspective. It was imperative for us here at the facility to grasp the concept that if we were to be passionate about the foodservice industry once we are released, our passion had to start now, while here incarcerated. The impact of this program is real. Personally, I believe I found my niche and have created a reentry program that was birthed only by my exposure to Today's Food Service Workforce Mentorship Program. In this book, Dr. Nugent has provided information that taps into the minds of those who read it and have presented us with tools to springboard us to success if we are willing to put in the work.

Wesley Ellis, Jr.
Mentor, Coach, and Facilitator
Wilkinson County Correctional Facility

Dr. Nugent brings insight into the complementary roles that individuals re-entering society and the food service industry can benefit from. She has developed a program that acknowledges the industry's need for a trained and eager workforce and marries it with formerly incarcerated individuals' need for redemption and self-worth. I look forward to weaving the threads from her newest book into the daily training at our facilities.

Laura Reid
State Director of Food Services
Mississippi Department of Corrections

Foodservice in corrections provides hands-on experience that builds confidence and career skills. It's a steppingstone for individuals to transition into the workforce with a strong sense of skills like food preparation, inventory management, sanitation, and teamwork. Mississippi prisons today have incarcerated residents trained to be restaurant managers upon release.

Derrick Chambers
Director – JCSWP, Private and Regional Facilities

Kim has taken her exceptional guide for thriving in the food service industry and adapted it to help those incarcerated learn industry skills and earn certifications. Their success and positive results validate their knowledge as they transition back to society. I applaud Kim for developing this important curriculum and mentoring program and greatly appreciate the growing number of corrections facilities who are stepping up to provide this service for their population. I know first-hand that those who reenter the workforce with training and confidence have a very strong chance to succeed.

Joe Kolenda
Principal Guthrie Center

Good quality food is essential in the daily management of residents in our prisons, and this starts with our food service team. As a Warden for over 20 years, our food service staff are often overlooked until we have an emergency. At that point, everyone realizes food service staff and residents' significant role. Creating programming opportunities that include mentorship to prepare incarcerated men and women with a strong career focus upon release is essential.

Scott Middlebrooks
Retired Warden, Federal Bureau of Prisons

TABLE OF CONTENTS

PURPOSE

To help incarcerated men and women find meaningful careers in the foodservice industry post-release:

- Inspire the latest ideas for recruitment when you are the manager/owner
- Share strategies for retaining key talent
- Provide a structured mentoring approach to build on employability skills
- Practice using career development tools prerelease
- Create a post-release reentry plan

INTRODUCTION

Do you ever take time to reflect on how you got into working in the kitchen while in prison? Maybe you had no previous experience, but now you find you are really good at it. If this sounds like you, this can be a great career when you are released. Why did you get into food service?

Maybe it was before prison when you cooked with your grandmother? Or was it your first job in high school? Maybe it was the smiles you received when you served someone a meal or a family came in to celebrate a special occasion, and you were hooked.

Was it a mentor who made a real difference and offered personal and professional life lessons? Was it a teacher? After your first career, did you decide it was time to pursue your passion later in life? However you got here, we are grateful.

Would you like to share your excitement with others and help them find their way into food service as a career instead of a steppingstone to some other place? We hope to help you get there. We believe this is a toolkit for success.

Segments of the Industry

The adventure of being in the food service industry is divided into segments. These include full service, quick service, eating and drinking, and retail host. Food service operators are across all industries, from retail shopping malls and hospitals to fine dining and vending machines. Food trucks, country and fitness clubs, airlines, ships, catering, event management, cafeterias, and franchises such as Chef for Seniors or Chick-fil-A all fit within the industry.

Employment opportunities are vast because the industry is so multifaceted. If you love food, you may find yourself looking to make a career in this industry. Traditional positions range from:

baker or pastry artist	banquet manager	bartender	broiler cook
cake decorator	dish washer	deli manager	barista
bus person	counter server	prep cook	sous chef
chef	executive chef	dining room manager	food truck
catering manager	retail grocery manager	butcher	sushi chef
sommelier	restaurant manager	delivery driver	waiter
hospitality manager	event planner	kitchen manager	dietician
hotel manager	owner-operators	line cook	host/hostess

and more (Indeed, 2021). Each job has its own set of responsibilities and requirements, so it is important to find a role that aligns with your skills and interests.

As the industry changes, so do job opportunities. According to Alison Doyle (2022), the top cool food jobs are food truck owner, food stylist, farmers market manager, craft brewer, holistic health coach, mushroom forager, restaurant designer, urban farmer, and vegan chef. As industry trends evolve, we need to upskill daily to stay competitive.

A Case Study: From Incarceration to Culinary Innovation: Transforming Lives Through Food Trucks

Many formerly incarcerated individuals face significant barriers to reintegration after serving their sentences, especially in the job market. However, for those with food service experience gained while in prison, an exciting and fulfilling career path awaits: the world of food trucks.

Jake's Journey: Could This Be You?

Jake, a former inmate, discovered his passion for cooking while participating in a culinary training program during his incarceration. He honed his skills in various aspects of food preparation, from basic knife techniques to advanced culinary arts. Upon his release, Jake faced the daunting challenge of finding employment with a criminal record. Traditional restaurant jobs were hard to come by due to the stigma attached to his past.

Jake decided to leverage his culinary talents and entrepreneurial spirit by starting his own food truck business. This decision not only provided him with a source of income but also allowed him to create a positive identity for himself in the community.

Steps to Success: Things You Need to Know

1. Business Planning: Jake took advantage of resources offered by local reentry programs, which provided guidance on business planning, permits, and financing. He developed a solid business plan focusing on a unique concept that combined his love for southern comfort food with healthy, locally sourced ingredients.

2. Support Network: Jake connected with nonprofit organizations that support formerly incarcerated individuals. These organizations helped him secure a small loan and provided mentorship to navigate the complexities of starting a business.

3. Building a Brand: With the help of his mentors, Jake crafted a brand that resonated with his story. He named his food truck Second Chance Eats, highlighting the themes of redemption and fresh beginnings.

4. Community Engagement: Jake actively engaged with his community, participating in local farmers' markets, food festivals, and charity events. This built his customer base and fostered a sense of belonging and purpose.

5. Continuous Learning: Jake remained committed to learning and improving his craft. He attended culinary workshops and kept up with food industry trends to ensure his menu remained innovative and appealing.

Impact and Growth

Jake's food truck quickly gained popularity, and he expanded his business by adding more trucks and hiring staff—many of whom were also formerly incarcerated individuals. By providing them with employment and mentorship, Jake created a ripple effect, helping others in similar situations rebuild their lives.

Conclusion

The story of Jake and Second Chance Eats illustrates the transformative power of food truck businesses for formerly incarcerated individuals with food service experience. These mobile kitchens offer a viable path to financial independence and serve as a platform for personal growth and community reintegration. Through perseverance, support, and a commitment to excellence, individuals like Jake can realize their culinary dreams, proving that everyone deserves a second chance.

Careers for Ex-Offenders

1. Restaurant Jobs: Positions such as dishwashers, prep cooks, line cooks, and servers are often available in felony-friendly restaurants like McDonald's, Pizza Hut, and Denny's.

2. Bartending: Some bars and pubs are open to hiring individuals with felony records, especially if the conviction is not related to alcohol or violence.

3. Housekeeping: Hotels and resorts often hire housekeepers, room attendants, and laundry staff, providing opportunities for those with felony records.

4. Food Truck Operations: Running or working in a food truck can be a great option for those with culinary experience.

5. Event Staff: Positions such as banquet servers, event coordinators, and catering staff are available in various event management companies.

6. Delivery Services: Companies like Uber Eats, DoorDash, and Postmates hire delivery drivers, which can be a good option for those with felony records.

7. Café Staff: Working as a barista, cashier, or kitchen staff in cafes and coffee shops can be a viable option.

8. Custodial Work: Hotels, restaurants, and event venues often hire custodial staff to maintain cleanliness and hygiene.

9. Kitchen Staff: Positions such as prep cooks, dishwashers, and kitchen assistants are available in many restaurants and catering companies.

10. Retail Positions: Some hospitality-related retail stores, such as those selling kitchenware or party supplies, may hire individuals with felony records.

These jobs provide opportunities for individuals with felony records to reintegrate into the workforce and build a positive future.

Pretend for a moment you are a food service employer. How would you answer, "What are the benefits of being in this industry?" Your future employees and mentees will want to know, so be ready to answer.

_____

_____

According to the Trade Schools, Colleges, and Universities newsletter (September 19, 2020), some of the exciting benefits of joining this truly diverse industry are:

- Opportunities for Career Progression: Most managers and owners started at the entry level in the industry within a segment and worked their way up based on their passion and interests.
- Versatile and Transferable Career Skills: You can enhance your communication, problem-solving, and customer service skills in this industry. Over time, you can become more organized and efficient, and these skills are transferable throughout the industry. Use your time in prison as the dress rehearsal for your life. Any issues that come up in prison will be there post-release, so let's start working on making positive changes now.
- Stimulating Social Interaction: You can interact with a wide variety of diverse people and even develop friendships at work.
- Free or Discounted Food: All food service operators have different policies regarding food discounts or a free meal when on shift. This discount or free meals can be a big money saver if you are new in the workforce.
- Desirable Health Benefits and Other Perks: Some companies provide health care benefits, education assistance, free coffee, juice, or soft drinks, and discounts within the community.

As we gain more experience and grow in our lives, sometimes we forget what it is like to be young or just starting out and even what drew us into this industry. It is always essential to start with *why* we do what we do in this industry and how it can benefit the employee, operation, and community.

Research on Today's Workforce Post-COVID

The genie is out of the bottle, which happened during the two-and-a-half years of the pandemic. We are not going back to the ways things used to be. While the research is not entirely clear on how many restaurants succumbed to the pandemic, entirely or temporarily, it certainly changed many things as we knew them. New public health restrictions were enforced, customer anxiety heightened, and operator debt increased (Carman, 2022). For those operators who weathered the storm, it seems they have returned stronger than ever. Customers wanted the opportunity to dine out and craved social interaction, even if large gatherings were restricted. During this time, food service operators had to be creative to stay open; this included delivery and packaging options, PPE precautions, social distancing, marketing, taking care of one another as operators, and so much more. However, as operators gained fluency in the new operating world, we would face a new problem that we might not have expected—a staff shortage.

At the same time, the workforce was reevaluating their lives when they lost friends and family members to COVID. What some call the Great Resignation is when employers saw one of the most significant changes in workforce history from resignations, retirement, and rethinking.

Employees genuinely thought about what they were doing: Were they working purposefully? Was their work making a difference? Was it making them happy?

Post-pandemic, our research says the workforce wants to work purposefully and know that what they do makes a difference. A new motivating factor for younger workforce members is for the employer to provide coaching, mentoring, and training at work to mirror how they have grown up. They want career advancement opportunities, whether vertical or hierarchical. They want to be listened to and given an opportunity to provide ideas regardless of age. They want flexibility at work, in scheduling, and in the use of technology.

As an employer, it will take innovative thinking to consider four-hour schedules or job sharing so you can appropriately staff while offering younger generations more flexibility to have a work-life balance. As an operator, it might require a shift in mindset. If you do not at least consider new options and your answer is "no" when asked about flexibility, you might have difficulty attracting the right talent for your operation.

Every generation wants to be appreciated and recognized, which is even more true with Generation Y or Millennials (born 1981–1996) and Generation Z (born 1997–2012). If you think your employees have a job and paycheck and that is enough, think again. Millennials and Generation Z make up most of today's workforce, and they are different. It is vital to keep up with the latest trends to be a competitive employer, or soon, you will be out of business.

If you are a Baby Boomer (born 1946–1964) or Generation X (born 1965–1980), you will find the workforce challenging and need to find new ways to adapt. By the time you are released, you might be working with Generation Alpha (born 2013–2024). If so, you may need a refresher on generations.

Today's workplace presents many challenges based solely on meeting goals, business objectives, and project deadlines. Throughout normal business activities, there are dynamics that could present issues and conflicts if left unchecked.

Since many older workers remain on the job longer and younger workers enter the workplace right out of high school or college, the work environment fragments into various generations. It is necessary to understand what generations are present in today's workplace to understand this diverse environment.

A generation is a group of people born during the same period who share the same attitudes and values, world events, and technological changes. The period is the factor in dividing the generations into groups. The five generations mentioned in the previous section have time ranges that define their period.

The Traditionalist Generation represents people in a generation born before 1946. The Baby Boomers are people born between 1946 and 1964. Generation X represents people born between 1965 and 1977, and Generation Y (Millennials) represents people born between 1978 and 1992. Generation Z represents people born after 1993.

In each period, there are experiences that shaped the attitudes and values of each generation. In addition, the interaction between generations is a factor in shaping the subsequent generation. For Millennials, events include the fall of the Berlin wall, Y2K, Hurricane Katrina, September 11, the Virginia Tech shooting, Barack Obama becoming President, the Royal wedding, and same-sex marriages becoming legal (Beausoleil, 2020).

Later, the pandemic was a world event that shaped Millennials' new way of thinking. Millennials want purpose, feedback, work-life balance, and recognition (Pfau, 2016).

DeFelice (2019) writes that employers make the mistake of thinking Gen Z is just Millennials plus, but they would be wrong. One world event that shaped Gen Z was the financial crash in 2008, where their families lost jobs, retirements, etc. (DeFelice, 2019). Generation Z wants stability, consistency, and connection through face-to-face and digital interaction, craves feedback, and expects diversity, equality, inclusion, sustainability, and appreciation. According to DeFelice (2019), this generation wants flexibility and trust in their work, not necessarily in scheduling.

Generation Alpha has seen technological advancements, the COVID-19 pandemic, climate change awareness, social movements such as Black Lives Matter and Me Too, cultural diversity and inclusivity valued, and economic shifts. Generation Alpha wants technological integration, sustainability and environmental action, inclusivity and diversity, mental health awareness, personalization and customization, global connectivity, and innovative learning. Because humans live an average of eighty-plus years, five potential generations may exist in the workplace today.

The five generations that exist today are:

- Baby Boomers
- Generation X
- Generation Y or Millennials (the majority of the workforce today)
- Generation Z (just entering the workforce and will become the majority soon)
- Generation Alpha (not in the workforce until 2028 or later)

From reading this section of the book, what shifts would you say are changing for employees, given the current state of the workforce?

_____

How is this different from how you see work?

_____

How is this different from being in prison right now?

_____

How are you keeping yourself on top of the trends and continuing to learn so you can adapt?

_____

This is one area in which you cannot ever stop learning.

Let's now focus on why people stay in their jobs. There are four categories: social ties, purpose, pay and prospects, and inertia. According to Matthews (2022), there are sixteen areas under the four categories to retain your employees. They are:

Social Ties

- A strong, supportive manager who mentors
- Relationships with coworkers
- Leadership they trust
- Feeling included

Purpose

- Belief in the company's mission and vision
- Satisfying and fulfilling work
- Cultural affiliation to the company
- Emotional investment in the company

Pay and Prospects

- Fair pay
- Chance to grow and be developed
- Feeling appreciated and recognized
- Clear career path

Inertia

- Job security
- Convenience
- Nothing better elsewhere
- Golden chains

We believe this book is the key to reimagining what is possible for our workforce's future in recruiting and retaining talent while creating a sustainable mentoring program and finding new ways to learn together.

A Recipe for Success

Recruiting

I believe you will one day find yourself employed in the food service industry and eventually become a hiring manager; then what? You might not see that as a possibility right now, but let's get you prepared.

According to Gordon Food Service (2022), finding strong candidates is half the battle. So, how do you do that in today's workforce and climate? "Each generation almost needs to be treated differently," says Karla Spaeth, department chair of Hotel, Restaurant, and Report Management at Northwood University in Michigan. The current workforce consists of Baby Boomers (born 1946–1965), Gen X (born 1966–1976), Millennials (born 1977–1992), and Gen Z (born after 1993).

Baby boomers are best reached the old-fashioned way through word of mouth, newspapers, Facebook (Meta), or career buttons on websites. For younger generations, social network pages are best. Examples are Snagajob.com, Craigslist.com, Kijiji.com, Twitter, and Instagram, to name a few. Industry-specific sites, like nutritionjobs.com, work for skilled positions.

As with every industry, food service operators had to reinvent new recruiting strategies during and after the pandemic. With fewer people on staff, operators are turning to technology and automation to become more agile (Schmidt, 2022).

Before you recruit, map out the ideal candidate. Create job descriptions to set expectations. Are you intentional about recruiting a diverse workforce?

Standard recruiting options are always available through LinkedIn, Indeed, Zip Recruiter, Career Builder, Monster.com, Simply Hired, Workforce Solutions, or local area marketing. The problem is that every operator is using these, and you are competing for the same great next hire.

Foodservice operators are improving the candidate experience by using AI technology platforms such as Paradox.ai, Talroo.com, Interviewer.ai, honestjobs.com, and many more. With multiple touchpoints, we can now keep potential candidates engaged. Younger candidates also want mobile-friendly options to apply on their phones.

Start with networking. Identify at least ten people in your network you can reach out to, ask for their ideas on areas to recruit, and share the qualifications you are seeking. When mapping out the plan, include personal and professional contacts. Ask your current staff who are performing well; they may have friends who want the same opportunity. Staff members do not always think about the operation like the manager or owner. If possible, include some incentive if their contact is hired and stays at least ninety days.

Local area high schools, community colleges, and universities are wonderful places to promote your job openings (Bonaparte, 2022). Your business will give them an opportunity and employment to gain experience. If you are looking for a more mature or experienced person, college food service or hotel and restaurant management alumni associations are great resources. Your local, state, or national restaurant, hotel, or culinary associations related to your specific segment of the industry are also helpful.

Consider your local area mega-churches, which have many specific programs that may have just the right people you are looking for to fill that next position (Kolenda, 2022). Another option within local churches is the between-job ministries. This population was probably laid off and is extremely motivated to find employment while updating their resume, interviewing skills, and social image profile.

You can find opportunities when a local food service operation closes. Some options would be to set up group or individual interviews and be an employee to support out-of-work staff (Restaurantbusiness.com). Wordsmith your job posting to ensure it accurately describes the position and does not fall to the bottom of the site algorithm. Consider this example: cook/dishwasher. A broader description may appeal to a candidate who wants to grow, not just do one job, and have career advancement opportunities. Consider offering internships or attending job fairs.

Another place to find notable talent is referrals from local area hospitals, prisons, or retirement communities for those wanting to break into the food service industry.

Self-Reflection

If you were the hiring manager, how would you recruit potential employees?

_____

_____

_____

Interviewing

Every operator has shifted away from face-to-face interviews and hosts virtual events and initial interview screens. Hiring the right talent is the other half of the equation. Much of Chick-fil-A's success is because they hire hard (Salvaggio, 2022). Prior to interviewing a candidate, much preparation has gone into the process. Many companies have found that using a behavioral-based assessment or set of behavioral-based interview questions provides a more accurate description of the candidate and their transferable skills. If you have determined the traits of the ideal candidate, you can develop a set of behavioral-based questions and rating guides to provide the most objective criteria when deciding. Examples include customer service skills, honesty, integrity, work ethic, dealing with conflict, meeting deadlines, etc. The sequencing of the questions is as follows:

- Tell me about a time when you _____.
- What action did you take?
- What were the results?
- Share with me your ideal workplace/leader/manager.
- Give me an example of when there was a problem at work or school, and you fixed it.

If your operation does not use behavioral-based techniques, search the Internet for questions to get started and then develop your own based on the traits you are looking for.

According to Bizjournal.com (2018), behavioral-based interview questions provide up to an 87 percent change performance index and produce better results. Chick-fil-A often interviews the candidate three times. The first one can be a phone or initial interview, the second one a panel interview of colleagues, and the final interview with the hiring manager. Do you want to know a part of their success? They hire for attitude, behavior, and character, not technical knowledge; they can train that.

You may be so understaffed in this business that it is tempting to make that desperate hire. Think again. One bad hire can cost the operation in terms of lower morale, decreased productivity, loss of customers, and loss of engagement. Promote from within when possible. It sends a strong and positive message.

Self-Reflection

What did you learn from this section on the interviewing process?

_____

_____

_____

Retaining

Orientation and Onboarding: Understanding the Differences

Orientation is a crucial part of the onboarding experience. It introduces newly hired employees to their organization, job responsibilities, and the policies and procedures associated with the organization and their specific department. Orientation includes general and departmental orientation for new employees (content and length vary by organization).

Onboarding refers to the ongoing process of building engagement with a new employee. It starts with accepting the offer letter, continues through new employee general orientation and departmental orientation, and ends when the employee becomes fully established within the organization (depending on the role, up to one year). A successful onboarding experience includes role-specific training, consistent communication, and feedback between the new employee and his or her manager.

With each step of the process, it is imperative to debrief with leadership staff on what went well and what can be improved and document a continuous improvement process.

Using a Getting to Know You Guide or Employee Recognition Questionnaire upon hire is key. Here are some examples.

Getting to Know You Guide

Name:

Kitchen Position:

Before we get started, let's get to know each other. By answering each of these questions, you will examine your skills, traits, competencies, and abilities before we start the mentoring program so I can best support you.

What is your first memory of cooking or baking?

What interests you in the food service industry?

What is your favorite food?

How would you describe your ideal food service workplace? Name at least three things that are important to you.

What motivates you in your life?

Where do you see yourself in five years?

What life events have shaped you (from ages one to ten)?

What technology (if any) did you grow up with? What technology have you heard about but have no idea what it is and how to use it?

How do you relate to people older than you? Younger than you?

What concerns you?

What do you want to accomplish after completing the mentorship program?

How can a mentor support you?

What are your gifts?

_____ Customer service skills
_____ Soft skills (collaborator, initiative, open to feedback, love to learn, positive attitude, etc.)
_____ Smart
_____ Creative
_____ Foodservice/nutrition knowledge
_____ Organized
_____ Other_____

How do you learn best?

_____ Auditory (listening)
_____ Visual (seeing)
_____ Tactile-kinesthetic (hands-on)

What are three of your weaknesses?

1.
2.
3.

What is your preferred method of communication?

What do you do for your health and well-being?

What are some of your hobbies?

What podcasts do you listen to, or what do you watch on TV?

Employee Recognition Questionnaire

This form assists managers with their employee recognition efforts. Please complete and return the form to your manager.

1. **What work accomplishments or contributions would you appreciate being recognized for by your manager or supervisor?**

   Customer service   Consistent job performance

   Innovative ideas or processes   Collaboration or support of team

   Taking on extra responsibilities or special projects

   Other, please describe: _____

2. **What would you find meaningful as a way of being recognized for the work accomplishments or contributions listed above?**

   Verbal acknowledgment   Personal note or card

   Lunch with supervisor   Administrative leave with pay

   Other, please describe:

3. In what type of setting are you most comfortable receiving recognition?

Private

Public

Unit/small group

No preference

Other, please describe:

4. Please list some of your favorite things so your manager or supervisor can get to know you better. (Please fill in the blanks if applicable.)

Favorite drink _____

Favorite music _____

Favorite snack _____

Favorite flower _____

Favorite dessert _____

Favorite sports team _____

Favorite food _____

Favorite color _____

Other: _____

5. Please provide any additional information you would like us to know.

Another effective strategy is to conduct thirty-, sixty-, and ninety-day check-ins to ensure the employees get what they need to succeed.

Check-in Questions for Thirty, Sixty, and Ninety Days

Thirty Days

1. What were your first week's impressions?

2. Why did you decide to accept this job?

3. On a scale of one to ten (ten is the highest), where would you rank your enthusiasm level?

4. What do you think are some of the reasons we hired you?

5. What do you want to know more about?

6. I want you to be successful; therefore, what do you need more or less of from me?

7. What has been your home-life conversation regarding your job? Your coworkers? What do you talk to them about?

8. What additional resources do you need?

9. What do you perceive to be your most meaningful contribution to the department in your first thirty days?

10. What have you learned about or from your coworkers? (At this point, the assumption is that the new employee has had an opportunity to meet with each department member).

11. What questions do you have for me?

12. What information are you lacking at this point that I can provide?

Sixty-Days

1. Last month, you noted your enthusiasm level was ___. Has it changed, and if so, why? If it has not changed, what else is needed (to increase or maintain it)?

2. What fuels your energy?

3. What do you want or need to know more about?

4. Last month, you stated you needed more or less of _____ from me.

   a. Have I followed through on that need or want?

   b. If so, how has that worked out for you? If not, what do I need to do differently to ensure I am providing you with what you need or want?

   c. Is there anything else you need more or less of at this point?

5. Including and beyond the department, how do you feel about the working environment here?

6. Who else do you believe you need to meet to establish rapport or relationships relative to your responsibility?

7. How do you determine your success in your new role?

8. What are your thoughts on giving and receiving feedback?

9. Do you have any questions for me?

Ninety-Days

1. Where is your enthusiasm level?

2. Relative to your role/job:

    a. What keeps you up at night?

    b. What holds your interest during the day?

3. How satisfied are you with your current duties and responsibilities?

4. How do you perceive your role and contributions a year from now?

5. What does success look like a year from now, and how will you know (measure) you reached it? How will I know?

6. What can we (the department) do differently during the next year?

7. Are there things we could (need to) improve?

8. What are some of the reasons you like working in this department?

9. What have you learned so far that you did not know when you started?

10. Do you have any questions for me?

Communication

When you are in charge, schedule regular staff meetings to keep everyone informed. Consider sending out a Monday morning message that recaps the week's highlights, a success story, changes in procedures, any upcoming audits, etc. The more you communicate, the better for everyone. Information is power. If you do not create your communication plan, you will have gossip running the department.

Depending on the number of staff you manage and their locations, schedule a quarterly staff meeting at a minimum. If you do not schedule them, they will not happen. Make them informative, fun, and engaging. Make the meeting worth the employee's time. Schedule one-on-one coaching sessions with each direct report at least quarterly, if not bi-weekly.

How would you create an orientation and onboarding program if you were in charge?

_____

_____

_____

Empowering Growth and Development

Before we get started, we need working definitions. These terms are central to employees and employers, and creating a retention plan is the next step.

- Growth and development are transformational processes in which improvement happens in your emotional, intellectual, social, and spiritual state. It reflects a commitment to developing the whole person.
- Professional or career development opportunities help ensure employees' knowledge and skills stay relevant and current. These opportunities allow employees to master the competencies necessary to excel in their chosen professions.
- Bench strength refers to an organization's ability to immediately fill critical positions with a talented internal candidate.
- A growth mindset (for developing talent) is a leader's attitude about his or her role in developing employees and his or her beliefs about employees' willingness and ability to grow and learn.

Did you know that providing growth and development for your team members is critical for you to keep your top talent?

It is not surprising that failing to deliver on this is likely to be one of the strongest drivers for your high-potential employees to seek their development elsewhere.

Research

- A survey of over 1,200 high achievers, averaging thirty years old, revealed that 95 percent were engaged in regular job search activities.
- Dissatisfaction with the development available to workers was a strong factor in their decision to leave an organization.
- The lack of formal development was one of the most significant factors fueling early exit.
- Seventy percent of development comes from job experience, twenty percent from learning from other people, and ten percent through formal learning programs.

Offer a balanced menu of development opportunities to ensure you retain talent.

Creating a Menu of Options

Make a list of learning resources you are aware of that could aid your employees' growth:

The Organization's Resources:	
Education:	
Certifications:	
Books:	
Podcasts:	
Websites:	
Job Shadowing Opportunities:	
Cross Training:	
Networking/Mentoring/Buddy Opportunities:	
Task Force or Committee Involvement:	
Professional Organizations (Be Specific.)	
What Else?	

Other Resources to Consider:

Personal Improvement: *Opportunities that hone a leader's skills and improve individual effectiveness*	• Receive a 360-degree feedback experience (feedback from manager, peers, and employees). • Join the mentoring program as a protégé. • Participate in coaching. • Maintain a leadership journal. • Start a leadership reading club. • Volunteer in the community. • Volunteer for a diversity council. • Teach a course to their employees. • Teach a course at a local university. • Join Toastmasters. • Complete Dale Carnegie. • Volunteer to lead a team effort, project, or assignment. • Volunteer to conduct a special assignment. • Participate in interim recruitment, job fairs, or college visits. • Assist junior staff in formulating their development plans. • Read at least two books every month. • Observe a leader and identify what makes that person a good leader. • Complete self-analysis instruments, such as True Colors, Birkman, DISC, MBTI, emotional intelligence, or other style instruments; obtain feedback on results. • Join a professional association. • Attend conferences. • Subscribe to a related professional journal. • Present at a conference.
Open Enrollment Classes: *Sessions offered internally, externally, or on demand (such as podcasts)*	• Enroll in a single university course. • Identify and register for courses offered internally. • Attend an external executive education program. • Attend an internal executive education program. • Take targeted leadership classes. • Complete an advanced academic degree. • Take advantage of e-learning opportunities, such as webinars. • Listen to podcasts. • Read blogs and research wikis.

Informal or Daily Options: *Chances to experience short-term projects or processes that build skills without a great disruption in current job responsibilities*	• Participate in stretch assignments. • Play an acting role when the supervisor is away. • Serve as a mentor. • Volunteer for an interview or hiring panel. • Lead a new project. • Be a "buddy" to a new employee. • Work with an actively involved boss. • Request on-the-job training to perfect skills.
Experiential Job Assignments: *Long or short-term opportunities to experience diverse scenarios that allow the candidate to gain organizational knowledge and prepare for broader leadership roles*	• Tour other departments or locations. • Participate in an organization-wide Six Sigma team. • Lead a cross-functional team or task force. • Shadow a leader in another department. • Accept a job rotation. • Work at another location or department for some time. • Connect with others through structured networking.
External Opportunities:	• Work with career field mentors from other organizations. • Use sabbaticals. • Teach a class at a local campus. • Participate in loaned executive programs. • Volunteer with nonprofit organizations.

Adapted from ATD Creating Leadership Development Programs (Online) Certificate Program

Self-Reflection

How can you improve your growth and development opportunities for you and your staff?

_____

_____

_____

Conducting Stay Interviews

How do you get employees to stay and love it at your organization? Show them you care (Kaye & Jordan-Evans, 2008).

A stay interview is a positive, scheduled, structured, informal discussion a leader conducts with an individual employee to identify specific actions the leader can take to strengthen the employee's engagement and increase his or her likelihood of staying with the organization.

A stay interview is not a performance discussion.

Leaders should conduct one stay interview per employee each calendar year.

Do you know the top reasons employees quit their jobs? Why wait until they leave to find out? Become proactive and use stay interviews annually. Do you know the cost of losing one employee? It goes beyond the financial costs, including lower employee morale, loss of operational experience, more overtime paid, burnout of other staff, etc.

Three primary skills go into an effective stay interview. They are listening, note-taking, and probing questions.

- Listening is critical. Avoid distractions, such as your cell phone, computer, etc.
- The interview is your time to be *completely attentive* to the employees and what they say. Use open and positive body language and smile. Do not interrupt!
- Taking notes creates a record of this critical conversation for reference when you co-create the stay plan and show the employee their feedback matters.
- Probing is your ability to ask open-ended questions without commenting on what they say.

- **Do not feel the need to answer questions or solve problems during the stay interview.**

A stay interview is a scheduled twenty-to-thirty-minute meeting with an employee one-on-one. Put your phone away and avoid distractions. You can gather sample questions from the internet. Some of my favorite questions are:

- What are you thinking about as you are about to begin your work each morning? What are you excited about when you come to work each day?
- What skills and talents would you like to contribute every day?
- How are we fully utilizing your skills and talents in your role?
- What job factors are you passionate about?
- If you could learn one additional topic related to your job, what would it be?
- What kind of feedback is most helpful to you?
- How do you decide when it is safe to talk to a supervisor or coworker about something difficult?

The stay interview is a positive reset for you and the employee to reengage staff, learn from them, and listen. Conduct annually with each employee. Take notes and follow up.

How can you improve employee engagement?

_____

_____

_____

Creating a Culture of Recognition

Did you ever think you could start a recognition program from day one? Here are some ideas to get you started. Employees consistently rank recognition in the five stay factors within an organization. No one leaves an organization because they feel overappreciated, but the opposite is true. Do you ever hear your employees say how much they love what they do or how much they feel appreciated? Here are some ideas on what you can do:

Day One Recognition

- Offer to be an onboarding "buddy" for new employees.
- Have a welcome poster signed by the team on the first day.
- Do a first-day ecard from the manager and colleagues.
- Ensure the new employee's workstation has all the necessary tools and access.
- Introduce the new employee to everyone in the department.
- Take them to lunch.
- Ask how the job is going and offer help.

Additional Ideas for Recognition

- Recognition photo display in break areas
- Off-site team building
- Use team meetings or huddles to recognize milestones and achievements
- Candy bar with a special note
- Written email or framed certificate from the leadership team for meeting goals
- Start meeting out with a fun quote or quick YouTube video or music to change the energy—put thought into your meetings so they see you care
- Lunch and learns
- Virtual get-togethers
- End-of-year banquet or awards
- Send a thank-you letter once a candidate accepts your offer letter
- Have a welcome poster signed by the team on the first day
- Recognition in front of peers
- Send birthday, anniversary, and special-event ecards
- Handwritten notes

- Surprise the employee with a special treat or book, such as "You are a lifesaver" and a roll of Lifesaver candy
- Make your virtual meetings fun
- Host food days to celebrate
- Celebrate national days or weeks
- Employee competitions
- Cookies delivered to their house
- Traveling trophy
- Virtual bulletin board posting team achievements
- Pay-it-forward program
- Posting praise from a customer
- Have peers call out cheers for each other for accomplishments
- Ask your employees what they would like
- Track the team's wins
- Feature employee of the month
- Create a virtual wall of fame
- Give rewards that are career based, such as sending an employee to a leadership class or training or certification class
- Encourage mentoring, virtual or otherwise
- Create a virtual suggestion box
- Say "Thank you"

Self-Reflection

How can you build a culture of recognition?

_____

_____

_____

Reimagine the Future

The latest trends and research show significant differences between generations, from Generation Z to Baby Boomers, in our workforce. While it is easy to share the trends, operationally adjusting is the challenge. It is up to you to adjust to recognize and adopt new approaches for each generation in your organization. The conflict often arises due to negative assumptions and lack of knowledge. The younger generations see a mismatch between what they think a business should try to achieve and actual priorities (Pulver, 2021). Do you wonder why? Look at what they have seen while growing up, from the Enron scandal to the Bernie Madoff financial scandal and so much more. No wonder they are turned off!

It is crucial for the younger generation to see the purpose—what you do matters, culturally a great place to work, professional development opportunities to work and grow, and work-life balance (flexibility in scheduling). Of course, the manager and team members are key to creating a sense of belonging.

We might underestimate that they are free to leave when they do not think the workplace is fair. Think back to when you were nineteen or twenty-five; maybe you felt the same way and have forgotten now that you have experienced and learned so much in your career. They need you more than ever!

I started my career in food service at fourteen and eventually was able to take part in the DECA program. This experience allowed me to go to school half a day and work half a day during my junior and senior years. I stayed in the food service industry because I loved it; I loved the variety. I would not have stayed in food service if my manager had not become my mentor at sixteen. She helped me personally and professionally. She taught me how to cook and about the various functions of a kitchen. She had me invest in culinary books to continue to learn. She gave me feedback when I needed it and was going off-course. Her name was Barbara McDonald. She helped me see the beauty in what we did, no matter how menial. She invited me along each time she made a career move, and I always said yes. I worked in the front and back of the house, making me more well-rounded as a manager. Are you that kind of manager?

If you are, your employees are thriving. If not, reassess your leadership traits and see how you can shift.

If you're experiencing turnover, you need to know why your employees are leaving. Don't wait for the exit interview. Use the strategies shared so far. Long gone are the days of one-size-fits-all.

Self-Reflection

How can you improve your knowledge of generational differences and adjust your style?

_____

_____

_____

Gap Analysis for the Owner/Operator/Leader to Complete

Are you the problem or the solution?

Operational Questions:	On a scale of one to ten, with one being poor and ten being best in class	Action steps needed to close the gap
Are your mission, vision, and value statements memorable?		
Have you created the ideal candidate profiles?		
Are your job descriptions documented?		
Have you clearly defined expectations?		
Do you have a comprehensive hiring strategy?		
Are your salaries competitive? Do you have fair hourly rates?		
Do you have a strong benefits package?		
Do you allow employees to participate in interview panels?		
Do you have a pipeline of candidates/bench strength?		
Do you understand what is important to each generation and modify accordingly?		
Do you use behavioral-based interview questions/assessments?		

Do you have a formal orientation and welcoming process?		
Do you use an employee recognition questionnaire to determine what is important to the employee?		
Do you have an effective yearlong onboarding program?		
Do you assign a buddy for the first ninety days?		
Do you conduct thirty, sixty, and ninety-day check-ins?		
Do you have an effective and consistent communication plan?		
Do you provide education or certification financial support?		
Do you ask employees for their ideas?		
Do you have an official mentoring program in place?		
Is job shadowing offered?		
Are there advancement opportunities—career lattices/ladders?		
Do you offer flexible scheduling options?		
Do you conduct stay interviews annually (at a minimum)?		

Do you perform performance evaluations (quarterly or annually)?		
Are you addressing reskilling or upskilling to build new career pathways?		
Do you have an effective and accessible recognition program?		
Do you provide ongoing feedback?		
Do employees know they can talk to you?		
Have you created a culture of psychological safety?		
Do you offer upskilling opportunities to meet the demands of the future?		
Do you schedule one-on-one coaching meetings?		
Do you facilitate effective staff meetings?		
Do you find ways to have fun at work?		
Have you created a company retention plan and assessed it quarterly?		

Personal Leadership Self-Assessment Questions

	On a scale of one to ten, with one being poor and ten being best in class	Action steps needed to close the gap
As the leader, are you investing in yourself?		
Are you a mentor manager?		
Are you staying out front and analyzing trends on the cutting edge?		
How comfortable are you with addressing conflict effectively?		
Are you a leader your employees want to follow regardless of location?		
Can you delegate effectively to empower and grow your team members?		
Do you know yourself and your talents?		
How do you stay healthy?		
How do you keep yourself from getting discouraged as a leader?		
How do you stay abreast of new technology?		

Mentor Self-Assessment: Are You Ready to Be a Mentor Manager?

Good leadership requires empathy, which is your ability to connect and relate to your employees. According to Clint Pulver (2021), a mentor manager is "where the magic happens" (p.64–65). This includes high expectations and a high connection with employees. According to Pulver, employees give their mentor manager respect and loyalty and engage with their work and coworkers. The mentor manager looks for the employees' potential while building trust and asking questions along the way. So, how do you do that?

The second half of this book will provide a structured way to build trust, empathy, kindness, and care.

The purpose of mentoring is to provide you with a structured roadmap that can be used while in prison with a small group of four and after release with a new group of mentees. You will draw from personal career experience and professional excellence. Feedback and coaching skills are secondary.

1. What is your why or purpose for being a mentor?

2. Conduct a SOAR analysis of yourself as a mentor:

   - My strengths are
   - My opportunities are
   - My aspirations are
   - The results I want to achieve are

3. Motivation

   - What motivates you to take on mentoring?
   - Do you have the confidence and competence to be a mentor?
   - What is your vision of the best possible outcome?
   - Do you feel you can make a connection and build trust?
   - What obstacles might prevent you from reaching the mentee's goals?

4. List the action steps for how you will:

   - Communicate
   - Use your personal experience
   - Adapt resources to the mentee's learning style
   - Deal with resistance
   - Be involved

5. What are the new skills, knowledge, and attitudes needed to make this change?

   - Skills
   - Knowledge
   - Attitudes

6. Determine how you will acknowledge, recognize, and celebrate after the program.

7. How will you keep the momentum going?

8. Goal Setting:

   - What are the mentee's personal goals?
   - What is the mentee's motivation for life?

9. Initial Conversation Starters:

   - How is it going?
   - What did you accomplish this week?
   - What did you learn about yourself this week?
   - Catch me up.

Getting to know your mentee is essential for this relationship to work.

Communication Strategies

- Build connections and trust.
- Be empathetic.
- Use active listening.
- Explore options. There is plenty of time.
- Provide encouragement.
- Co-create opportunities.
- Acknowledge the effort they are putting in.

Facilitating/Asking Questions

The remarkable thing about this book is the questions have been created for you. You can certainly expand on them. However, we want to caution you about what is not helpful. We have found that these approaches are not useful in the mentoring relationship. Remember:

- You are not a therapist.
- Be a friend first before being a mentor. Developing a strong bond of trust is critical.
- Telling them everything you have done for the past twenty to forty years is not the focus.
- Asking questions is most helpful in this relationship. Sometimes, mentees are looking for answers, and that is when your experience can help guide them.
- Do not push your agenda.
- Do not solve their problems. The mentees need to solve problems for themselves. If there is a week when you feel the mentee is going in the wrong direction, pause the conversation. Ask the mentee to write their thoughts and what they want to ac-

complish and pick it up next week. You both need time to reflect. Do not push it if it does not feel right.

- Do not tell them what to do.

Feedback

- Do not ask why questions. It puts people on the defensive, and behaviors do not change. Once a relationship is established, your questions will come naturally.
- Begin discussions with how or what questions.
- Always be respectful of your mentee.
- Actively listen to what they say.

Problem Solving

Use this model to problem solve (Connellan, 2002):

- Define the issue.
- Explore options.
- Develop solutions.
- Reinforce positive ideas.
- Close the deal/gain agreements. Do not assume anything; ask for their commitment.

Reflection on Learning

- How are you doing?
- What is working?
- Where are you struggling, or what are you still confused about?

Structure

- Commit once a week to meet—be flexible.
- Decide where and how you will meet.
- Set the time and date.
- Take notes.
- Mentor relationships can be one-on-one, or a mentor can actively mentor small groups of up to four people.

Celebrate Learning/Rewards

- Thank-you notes
- Face-to-face acknowledgment

The research is clear that having a mentor in life is immensely helpful. While many organizations start mentoring programs, the programs rarely produce the intended result or merely do not remain active. To prevent this from happening, preparation is key.

Preparation and Expectations for the Mentor:

- Review and commit to the schedule.
- Read the chapter or article for the week.
- Review the self-assessment questions.
- Review the mentor questions.
- Think about how you can expand the conversation based on your goals and experience. Bring in additional resources.

"People will forget what you said, people will forget what you did, but people will never forget how you made them feel."

—Maya Angelou

Mentee-Mentor Agreement

We are both excited about embarking on this journey together. We want this to be a rewarding experience, spending most of our time discussing developmental activities that will provide valuable knowledge. We agree that:

1. The mentoring relationship will last for a minimum of six months. If it does not meet the mentee's needs, we can decide to end the formal relationship at any time through a conversation.

2. We will meet weekly. Once agreed upon, meeting times should not be canceled unless absolutely necessary. At the end of each meeting, we will agree on a date for the next meeting.

3. Each meeting will be sixty minutes.

4. We agree that the role of the mentor is to:

   - Provide guidance, share ideas, and provide feedback.
   - Function as a sounding board for ideas/concerns about life choices.
   - Identify resources to help enhance personal development and career growth.
   - Serve as an advocate for the mentee whenever the opportunity presents itself.

5. We agree that the role of the mentee (you, the learner) is to:

   - Identify the skills, knowledge, and goals you want to achieve and communicate with your mentor.
   - Maintain a mentoring plan and work with your mentor to set goals, developmental activities, and time frames.
   - Work with your mentor to see resources for learning; identify people and information that might be helpful.

6. We agree to keep the content of these meetings confidential.

7. The mentor agrees to be honest and provide constructive feedback to the mentee. The mentee agrees to be open to the feedback and say, "Thank you."

Date:_____

Mentor's signature: _____

Mentee's signature: _____

The Mentor Facilitation Workshop Schedule

Program Orientation
Forms
Book Review
Self-Reflection
Writing Activities
Getting to Know You Guide
Mentor Agreement
Self-Assessment
A to Z

Set the weekly schedule. Provide your contact information to the prison staff scheduler.

Set the schedule. Plan for 1.5 hours to allow time for the men or women to get into the classroom. The meeting may be delayed because of other priorities in the prison. You only need one hour per week for each session. You will mentor a small group of one to four people.

Share the weekly expectations with your mentees. You and the mentees need to be prepared to read the article, answer the questions, and take part in the discussion every week. Some weeks will require more homework.

The Timeline

Week	Mentor Topics	Assignments for the Next Week
Week 1	Getting to Know You Guide and Program Expectations	
Week 2	Overview, Self-Assessment, and Mentor/Mentee Agreement	Complete the Self-Assessment Inventory. Read A is for Attitude, interview five people, and complete the mentee questions.
Week 3	A is for Attitude	Discuss the article and mentor questions.

Week 4	B is for Brand	Discuss the article and mentor questions.
Week 5	C is for Communication	Discuss the article and mentor questions.
Week 6	D is for Diversity and Drive Performance	Discuss the article and mentor questions.
Week 7	E is for Energy	Discuss the article and mentor questions.
Week 8	F is for Foodservice	Discuss the article and mentor questions.
Week 9	G is for Gratitude	Discuss the article and mentor questions.
Week 10	H is for Hospitality	Discuss the article and mentor questions.
Week 11	I is for Integrity	Discuss the article and mentor questions.
Week 12	J is for Jaded	Discuss the article and mentor questions.
Week 13	K is for Knowledge Review the Career Development Tools section	Discuss the article and mentor questions. Complete the following: Application Exercise Functional Resume Proof of Education/Certifications Create a list of recommendations/references.

Week 14	L is for Life-Long Learner Review the resources at the end of the book to see what you need and do not have yet. Begin working on obtaining them. Determine what staff member at the facility can help you.	Discuss the article and mentor questions. Read the Now Hired Now What? section.
Week 15	M is for Mindset Discuss Now Hired Now What?	Discuss the article and mentor questions.
Week 16	N is for Nutrition O is for Opportunity	Discuss the article and mentor questions.
Week 17	P is for Problem Solver	Discuss the article and mentor questions.
Week 18	Q is for Question	Read the Career Development section about: Personal hygiene Practice the professional handshake Punctuality Interviewing The challenging questions Be ready to practice interviewing questions.
Week 19	R is for Revenue and Responsibility Discuss the Career Development assignment from last week	Discuss the article and mentor questions.
Week 20	S is for Serve Safe	Discuss the article and mentor questions.

Week 21	T is for Teamwork U is for Unique	Discuss the article and mentor questions.
Week 22	V is for Vision W is for White Lies	Discuss the article and mentor questions.
Week 23	X is for X-Factor Y is for Yearning	Discuss the article and mentor questions.
Week 25	Z is for Zone Complete the Self-Assessment for A to Z	Discuss the article and mentor questions. Read and review the Post-Release Checklist for Integration
Week 26	Complete the Post-Release Checklist and plan for integration Discuss the Post-Release Checklist and plan for integration	Discuss the following: "Develop the Ultimate Realistic Plan" Returning to what city? How will you get there? What family support do you have? What church home will provide support? Where will you live? What environment do you need to avoid so you don't return to prison? What programs do you need to access? What are you most concerned about?
Week 27	Segments of the Industry	Assignments for the Next week
Week 28	Recipe for Success Recruiting and Interviewing	Assignments for the Next week
Week 29	Retaining	Assignments for the Next week
Week 30	Now What—Next Steps	Design your life plan

Getting to Know You Guide

Name:

Kitchen Position:

Before we get started, let's get to know each other. By answering each of these questions, you will examine your skills, traits, competencies, and abilities before we start the mentoring program so I can best support you.

What is your first memory of cooking or baking?

What interests you in the food service industry?

What is your favorite food?

How would you describe your ideal food service workplace? Name at least three things that are important to you.

What motivates you in your life?

Where do you see yourself in five years?

What life events have shaped you (from ages one to ten)?

What technology (if any) did you grow up with? What technology have you heard about and have no idea what it is or how to use it?

How do you relate to people older than you? Younger than you?

What concerns you?

What do you want to accomplish after completing the mentorship program?

How can a mentor support you?

What are your gifts?

_____ Customer service skills
_____ Soft skills (collaborator, initiative, open to feedback, love to learn, positive attitude, etc.)
_____ Smart
_____ Creative
_____ Foodservice/nutrition knowledge
_____ Organized
_____ Other_____

How do you learn best?

_____ Auditory (listening)
_____ Visual (seeing)
_____ Tactile-kinesthetic (hands-on)

What are three of your weaknesses?

1.
2.
3.

What is your preferred method of communication?

What do you do for your health and well-being?

What are some of your hobbies?

What podcasts do you listen to, or what do you watch on TV?

Let's create a weekly schedule.

Day of the week:

Time of the week:

Preferred method:

Thank you for completing the Getting to Know You Guide.

Self-Assessment Inventory Instructions

What if we created a win-win situation? Let's begin by starting the self-assessment inventory. In the second column, rate yourself in each category from one to ten, one being poor and ten being excellent. Do not skip any of the twenty-six categories. Save the third column for your weekly coaching meetings.

If you are the mentor, schedule weekly coaching meetings. Read the questions before meeting with the employee to determine where you want to take the conversation. Feel free to ask questions based on your experience or food service culture. This approach will help you mentor a new generation of aspiring leaders and make a lasting impact on another's life. By using this approach, you are leaving a legacy for others to step into their future.

Pre Self-Assessment Inventory

	Rate yourself one to ten, one being poor and ten being excellent	Plan to improve/resources utilized
Attitude		
Brand		
Communication		
Diversity and Drive Performance		
Energy		
Foodservice		
Gratitude		
Hospitality		
Integrity		
Jaded		
Knowledgeable		
Lifelong Learner		
Mindset		
Nutrition		
Opportunity		
Problem Solver		
Question		
Revenue and Responsibility		
Serve Safe		
Teamwork		
Unique		
Vision		
White Lies		
X-Factor		
Yearning		
Zone		

> *"A positive attitude gives you power over your circumstances instead of allowing your circumstances to have power over you."*
> —Joyce Meyer

How essential is having a positive and professional attitude at work? What is your attitude each day when you arrive at your work assignment? Do you maintain a positive attitude throughout the day? Do people like to be around you? Do you bring a positive outlook to the workspace, or do people avoid you? What is your attitude when things do not go your way? What is your attitude when things you want are delayed? How do you handle it? What are your attitude triggers in prison? What is one step you can take to improve your attitude? Prison is the dress rehearsal for life when you are released. Whatever bothers you in prison will still bother you when you are released, so why wait? Begin transforming your life now!

Do you bring down the team? Do people make excuses for you, such as saying, "Well, that is just the way he or she is," and try to avoid you? Are you an energy drain on the team? Do not be a Debbie Downer or a Ned Know It All.

After authoring his book, *The Energy Bus*, Jon Gordon wrote an article called "How to Deal with Energy Vampires." You do not want to be known as an energy vampire—someone who sucks the air out of the room. Others feel bored, overwhelmed, and frustrated when they are around them. These people exist. Make sure you are not one of them. Remember, bad attitudes are contagious, and so are good ones. How would people you work with describe your attitude?

According to the dictionary, the definition of attitude is a way of thinking or feeling expressed through behaviors. You can express your attitude in various ways, such as job satisfaction, productivity, innovation, respect, helpfulness, and overall morale within the department.

Attitude is fundamental to your career success. It is known as a soft skill. There are many excellent ways to find out about your attitude to form a baseline if you do not feel you are as self-aware as you would like. We all have blind spots, and you cannot uncover them by yourself. Assessments can include attitude, emotional intelligence, leadership skills, etc. We all have blind spots, so the more you discover yours by asking others around you and then taking action steps to improve, the more confident and promotable you become.

Start each day with a gratitude journal or positive meditation or affirmations. The more consistent you are with starting each day like this, the more your attitude will improve. Taking small steps each day creates more significant attitude opportunities. Once you find beauty in the little things, your universe expands in proportion.

Surround yourself with positive people. Don't you love being around positive people? Positive people inspire and motivate me. They make me smile. Do you make others smile?

Do excellent work without expecting anything in return. Be willing to forgive. Learn from your mistakes, and do not beat yourself up mentally. When you make a mistake, get in the habit of thinking through what you learned and then move on. Do not dwell on negative things, people, or conversations. Part of my professional success is that I do not dwell on problems. I take action and work to find solutions. I advise taking action; a change in attitude will follow.

Charles R. Swindoll is well known for his quote on attitude. He says, "Life is 10 percent what happens to you and 90 percent how you react to it." We can change our attitudes. He said that the longer he lives, the more he realizes how imperative attitude is. It is more important than facts, past education, money, circumstances, appearance, skills, or what other people say and do. It will make or break a company, family, relationship, or church. We must choose our attitude every day.

John C. Maxwell authored *Attitude 101: What Every Leader Needs to Know*. This book is a practical guide and a wonderful place to start examining your thoughts, feelings, and behaviors at work. Maintaining a positive attitude can determine your circumstances, energize the team, and take your first step toward leadership. It starts with you.

Self-Assessment Questions

Questions	Responses
How self-aware are you?	
Have you ever taken an attitude assessment? Let's create a 360-degree attitude assessment. Interview five people. Here is the assignment.	
If you were to ask your pod mates about your attitude, what would they say? Interview five people you trust who will give you direct feedback about your attitude.	
What would your correctional staff say regarding your attitude? If you do not know, ask.	
What would your chaplain or teachers say about your attitude?	
What would the kitchen manager say about your attitude?	
What would your family say about your attitude?	
How do you respond when you hit an attitude roadblock at work?	

Do you feel you are resilient? If yes, give an example.	
How do you get back on track if you get off track?	
Provide an example of when you chose a positive attitude in a stressful situation.	
In what area do you think you excel?	
What is one area in which you could improve your attitude?	
What is one action step you can take to improve in this area?	
How will you know you are making progress?	

Coach/Mentor Questions

Describe your attitude self-assessment.	
Did you ask others for feedback about your attitude?	
Did you learn anything new?	
Did any comments surprise you?	
What is one action step you can take to improve your attitude?	
How will you measure your improvement in this area?	
How can I support you?	
Assignment for Next Week:	

B IS FOR BRAND

> *"Your brand is what people say about you when you are not in the room."*
> —Jeff Bezos, Amazon

Brand is so much more than dressing for success. It is everything you do every minute of the day. Think of a brand as your portfolio: Me, Inc. What does your brand say about you? What impression do you think you are making daily? Are you consistent? Your brand includes how you dress, communicate, and carry yourself. It is your content defined by your expertise and unique humanity: generosity, vulnerability, accountability, and candor (Ferrazzi & Raz, 2005). Your brand is your walking billboard of everything you do, communicate, project, and wear. Until now, you might not have ever thought about your brand. Guess what? Other people can describe your brand whether you know it or not. Now, it is time to be intentional about your brand.

A brand is a way of personally marketing yourself in your career. So, you must be self-aware before you can build your brand in person and through social media. As you develop your career, you want to be known as someone people can count on. Developing a positive brand while working in a prison kitchen can be a transformative experience for an inmate. Here are some steps to help achieve this:

1. Embrace the Opportunity

   - Take the Initiative: Show enthusiasm and dedication in your work. This can set you apart and show your commitment to personal growth.
   - Learn and Improve: Take advantage of any culinary training programs or workshops offered. Continuously seek to improve your skills and knowledge.

2. Build Relationships

   - Collaborate with Others: Work well with your fellow inmates and kitchen staff. Positive relationships can lead to recommendations and support.
   - Seek Mentors: Find experienced inmates or staff who can provide guidance and mentorship.

3. Create a Positive Reputation

- Consistency: Be reliable and consistent in your work. This builds trust and a positive reputation among your peers and supervisors.
- Show Respect: Treat everyone with respect and professionalism. This can help you gain respect in return.

4. Develop a Unique Skill Set

- Specialize: Focus on developing a unique skill set, such as specializing in a particular type of cuisine or cooking technique.
- Innovate: Bring creativity to your work. Experiment with new recipes or ways to improve existing dishes as allowed.

5. Document Your Journey

- Keep a Journal: Document your progress, recipes, and any new skills you learn. This can serve as a portfolio to showcase your work.
- Share Your Story: If possible, share your journey through social media, other platforms, or the prison newsletter. This can help build your personal brand and connect with a wider audience.

6. Prepare for Reentry

- Network: Build connections with people in the prison who can help you find employment opportunities upon release.
- Plan Ahead: Start planning for your reentry into society by researching job opportunities and potential employers who are open to hiring individuals with felony records.

By following these steps, you can develop a positive brand and set yourself up for success inside and outside prison.

Once you are released and have access to social media, think about where you post and what you post. What would your employer say about these posts? Would they believe you demonstrate company values? Or would they think they had made an unwise decision hiring you? Your social media brand is your digital fingerprint and follows you throughout your career.

Your posts can help or harm your career. Some prospective employees were not offered positions because of Facebook and other social media postings. Examples of such posts are Saturday night bar shots, foul language, provocative dress, etc. Nothing is off the record. Big Brother is watching regardless of your privacy settings.

On the other hand, other employers hired some prospective employees because of their strong brands, posts, and contributions on their social media accounts. Examples of posts include professional photos, family outings, and volunteer work at a food bank, Habitat for Humanity, etc. These demonstrate strong values.

LinkedIn is the most effective business tool. Once released, take the time to build your profile. Learn how to do this. There are books, online resources, other LinkedIn profiles, and LinkedIn University to help you. Do you have a professional photograph for your social media accounts? Is your resume updated? How strong are your connections? How did you invite them? How many groups do you belong to? What videos, articles, or pictures are you posting/sharing? Do you have a strong headline? Do you blog or post so you can become a food service or customer service thought leader? Do you have solid recommendations for you on your LinkedIn profile? These recommendations on LinkedIn can enhance your career visibility opportunities. Choose wisely when asking for professional recommendations. Recommendations may be from a teacher, former employer, correctional staff leaders, chaplain, etc.

Many years ago, I worked for an organization as president of one of the operating units. The president of the parent corporation was leaving, and I knew him well. He knew my work well. I asked him for a LinkedIn recommendation when I was setting up my profile. Honestly, I never thought about it again. Fast forward six years; I had left my company and was interviewing for a new position with a new company. The company flew me to Chicago for a face-to-face interview. While waiting, the Human Resources recruiter met and talked with me. She first said, "I checked out your LinkedIn profile." She told me, "You have impressive recommendations." I had forgotten about those recommendations. The man interviewing me for the new position with the new company was the former president of the parent corporation I had worked for many years ago. It was evident that this recommendation helped me get an interview. Oh, and yes, I got the job.

Beyond social media is your brand at work. How do you show up? Are you helpful? Do you consistently do your best work? Do you dress in a clean uniform every day? Do you shower daily and use deodorant? Do you get regular haircuts and shave?

No one can be an expert in everything, so ask questions. Seek more experienced people and learn from them. Seek thought leaders and see what they are doing. You are unique, so capitalize on your strengths.

There are so many great places to seek how to improve your brand. In 2004, *Fast Company* featured the article "The Brand Called You" written by Tom Peters. To deepen your understanding, check out this article to learn how you can improve your brand: https://www.fastcompany.com/28905/brand-called-you. Your brand is your reputation every day.

Self-Assessment Questions

Interview five people about your brand and take notes. How do they describe your brand to you? What does your brand communicate about you? How can you improve?	
Before this activity, what would people say about you if you were not in the room?	
How self-aware are you, one being poor and ten being excellent?	

On a scale of one to ten, how strong is your brand?
 	
  a. Face-to-face
 	
  b. Communication
 	
  c. Work ethic
 	
  d. Knowledge in the kitchen
 	
  e. Social media accounts	

What is one area in which you could improve your brand in the kitchen or work assignment?	

When you have access to social media, how could you improve your brand by setting up social media accounts? Is there anything you have posted in the past that might have you concerned?	
How will you learn more about developing your brand?	
What is one action step you can take to improve your brand?	
How will you know you are making progress?	

Coach/Mentor Questions

Describe your brand's self-assessment.	
What did you learn about your brand that you have never thought about before?	
Did you ask others for feedback on your brand? What did you learn?	
Did you ask others for feedback on your social media accounts?	
Did you learn anything new?	
Did any comments surprise you?	
What is one action you can take to improve your brand?	
How will you measure your improvement in this area?	
How can I support you?	
Assignment for Next Week:	

> *"The art of communication is the language of leadership."*
> —James Humes

Effective communication is key to building strong relationships and succeeding in any environment, including prison. It involves listening to understand others fully and presenting information clearly using oral, written, visual, and nonverbal skills. Here are some steps to help you improve your communication skills while in prison so you are ready for release.

Assess Your Communication Skills

- Listening: Do you listen to understand or just to respond? Practice active listening by focusing on the speaker and avoiding interruptions.
- Speaking: Are you able to convey your thoughts clearly? Practice speaking confidently and concisely.
- Writing: Are your written communications clear and appropriate? Use tools like spellcheck and Grammarly to improve your writing.
- Nonverbal Communication: Be aware of your body language and facial expressions, as they convey a lot of information.

Enhancing Your Skills

1. Listening Skills:

   o Listen, Don't Talk: Focus on understanding the speaker.
   o Avoid Interruptions: Let the speaker finish before you respond.
   o Ask Questions: Clarify points to ensure you understand correctly.

2. Speaking Skills:

   o Practice Public Speaking: Join groups like Toastmasters International, which may have chapters in some prisons.

o Build Confidence: Organizations like Dale Carnegie Training offer strategies to improve public speaking and confidence.

o When you want to change a behavior. The word "Why" is not an effective way to start. It puts people on the defensive. Change the word Why to "What or How" Ex: Why did you do that - puts people on the defensive. Instead, say How did that happen? or What happened?

o Change starting a sentence with You to I Ex: You made me angry puts people on the defensive. Instead, say that yesterday, when we talked, I felt angry. They may not like what you said, but the person cannot argue with our feelings.

3. Writing Skills:

o Practice Regularly: Write letters, emails, or journal entries to improve your writing.

o Use Tools: Utilize spellcheck and grammar tools to refine your writing.

4. Nonverbal Communication:

o Be Mindful: Pay attention to your body language and facial expressions.

o Practice: Use a mirror or record yourself to see how you come across.

Resources for Improvement

- Dale Carnegie Training: Great for beginners and introverts, offering public speaking and confidence-building strategies.
- Toastmasters International: Helps practice speaking skills; some prisons have chapters, and you can join a local chapter after release.
- National Speakers Association (NSA): For those aspiring to be professional speakers or leaders.

Tips for Better Listening

- Listen, don't talk
- Avoid interruptions
- Ten percent talking
- Related conversation
- Do not offer advice
- Be aware of your environment
- Take notes if required

Overcoming Communication Barriers

- Mehrabian Communication Model: Remember that 93 percent of communication is nonverbal (55 percent body language, 38 percent tone of voice).
- Cultural and Language Differences: Be mindful of these barriers and work to overcome them.

Self-Assessment and Improvement

- A–Attitude, B–Brand, C–Communication: Assess yourself in these areas and identify opportunities for improvement. These are foundational skills.
- Personal Development: Take classes and seek resources to continue improving your communication skills.

Focusing on these areas can enhance your communication skills, build better relationships, and prepare for successful reentry into society. Keep practicing and stay committed to your personal growth.

Self-Assessment Questions

Rate your communication on a scale of one to ten, with one being poor and ten being excellent.
 	
_____Listening
 	
_____Speaking
 	
_____Writing
 	
_____Presenting
 	
_____Facilitating
 	
_____Nonverbal communication
 	
    _____Body language
 	
    _____Tone of voice	

What is one area you need to start improving first?	
What is one area where you could improve your communication skills at work?	
What outside resources will help you improve in this area?	
Have you ever participated in Toastmasters, Dale Carnegie, National Speakers Association, or personal-development courses to improve communication?	
How will you know you are making progress in this area?	

Coach/Mentor Questions

Describe your communication skill strengths.	
Describe your communication skill weaknesses.	
How important are effective communication skills for your personal and professional lives?	
Have you ever participated in Toastmasters, Dale Carnegie, National Speakers Association, or personal-development courses to improve communication?	
What communication resources are you aware of that could be used to improve in this area? Please share.	
What is one action you can take to improve in this area?	
How will you measure your improvement in this area?	
How can I support you?	
Assignment for Next Week:	

D IS FOR DIVERSITY AND DRIVE PERFORMANCE

> *"What we can control is our performance and our execution, and that's what we're going to focus on."*
> —Bill Belichick

Diversity

Did you know that the food service industry is one of the most diverse segments of the economy (Connell, 2022)? According to the 2021 U.S. Department of Labor, half of all restaurant employees are minorities. The industry view is that this diversity is a strength because food service operators serve a diverse customer base.

What does diversity mean to you? There are dimensions of diversity. Primary attributes are race, gender, generation/age, mental/physical abilities, ethnicity, and sexual orientation. Secondary attributes are personality, income, education, profession, religion, values, parental or marital status, military experience, and skills (LinkedIn Learning, 2020).

How have you educated yourself to be culturally sensitive? How have you learned about other cultures, backgrounds, and generations? How are you continuing to improve your cross-cultural communication skills?

Learning about cultural diversity and becoming more respectful in prison is possible. Here are several strategies inmates can use to develop a greater appreciation for cultural differences and foster tolerance:

1. Education Programs

   - Cultural Awareness Classes: Many prisons offer educational programs focusing on cultural awareness and diversity. Enrolling in these classes can provide valuable insights into different cultures, traditions, and perspectives.
   - Language Learning: Learning a new language can open doors to understanding different cultures. Many facilities provide language courses or access to language-learning resources.

2. Reading and Research

- Books and Articles: Reading books, articles, and essays about different cultures and histories can broaden an inmate's understanding. Prison libraries often have diverse collections that can be valuable resources.
- Online Courses: If internet access is available, online courses on cultural studies, anthropology, and history can be highly beneficial.

3. Peer Interaction and Dialogue

- Engage in Conversations: Interacting with fellow inmates from diverse backgrounds can provide firsthand experiences and foster mutual understanding. Encouraging open and respectful dialogues can break down stereotypes and build empathy. Ask others about their families, foods they enjoy, activities, music, etc.
- Discussion Groups: Joining or forming discussion groups focused on cultural topics can provide a platform for sharing and learning from each other.

4. Participation in Cultural Activities

- Cultural Celebrations: Participate in or organize cultural events and celebrations within the facility. This can include sharing traditional foods, music, and customs from different cultures.
- Art and Music: Engaging in art and music from different cultures can be a powerful way to connect and appreciate diversity. Many prisons have art programs that allow inmates to explore different cultural expressions.

5. Mentorship and Counseling

- Seek Guidance: It can be beneficial to find a mentor or counselor who can provide guidance on cultural sensitivity and respect. Many prisons have programs where experienced inmates or staff offer support and mentorship.
- Self-Reflection: Counseling sessions focused on self-reflection and personal growth can help inmates understand their biases and develop a more inclusive mindset.

6. Volunteering and Service

- Community Service Projects: Participating in community service projects within the prison, such as organizing donation drives or educational workshops, can help inmates develop a sense of community and appreciation for diverse backgrounds.
- Peer Support Programs: Engaging in peer support programs that assist fellow inmates from different cultural backgrounds can build empathy and understanding.

7. Mindfulness and Self-Awareness

- Mindfulness Practices: Mindfulness and meditation can help inmates become more self-aware and develop a compassionate outlook toward others.
- Journaling: Keeping a journal to reflect on personal experiences, interactions, and lessons about cultural diversity can help one internalize these lessons and foster growth.

8. Post-Release Planning

- Prepare for Reentry: Planning for reentry by seeking diverse communities and support networks can help maintain the growth achieved in prison. Connecting with community organizations focusing on cultural diversity and inclusion can provide continued support.

By engaging in these strategies, inmates can develop a deeper understanding and respect for cultural diversity, preparing them for a more inclusive and tolerant life upon release. Remember, we all make value judgments; it is the nature of humans. However, work to set those aside, get curious, and learn about others and what you have in common.

Drive Performance

The definition of drive performance is to plan and execute work effectively to achieve performance goals. It also shows persistence in overcoming obstacles.

What is one thing you can do to at least meet expectations for driving performance while in prison? Upon release?

Self-Assessment

Instructions: Check the boxes that seem most like you. Add one check mark in each row. Where are the opportunities to improve your ability to drive performance?

Does Not Meet Expectations		Meets Expectations		Exceeds Expectations	
Is reluctant to push for results		Has a strong bottom-line orientation		Sets aggressive goals and has ambitious standards	
Does the least to get by		Persists in accomplishing objectives despite setbacks and obstacles		Is consistently one of the high performers	
Is an inconsistent performer		Has a history of successfully exceeding goals		Pursues everything with energy, drive, and the need to finish	
Often misses deadlines		Pushes self and helps others achieve results		Persists in the face of challenges and setbacks	
Procrastinates and lets obstacles get in the way				Always keeps the end in sight; puts in the extra effort to meet deadlines	
Total the check marks in each column					

Did you know there are benefits to driving your performance?

- Employees are motivated.
- You know your strengths and weaknesses.
- Employees are engaged.
- Employees understand their job responsibilities.
- Administrative actions are fair.

There are things you can do to improve your performance. They are:

- Ensure you understand the expectations.
- Seek continuous feedback; be coachable.
- Ensure you understand the organization's goals and how you can contribute.
- Know your strengths and areas of improvement.
- Measure your success and effort.
- Know the expected outcome.

Self-Assessment Questions

Questions	Responses
How have you educated yourself to be culturally sensitive?	
How have you learned about other cultures, backgrounds, and generations?	
How are you continuing to improve your cross-cultural communication skills?	
What did you learn about yourself from your self-assessment?	
What are some things you do to drive your performance?	
What are some benefits if we, as a team, can drive performance?	
What is one area of improvement for you when you think about driving performance?	
Do you ever have a problem consistently delivering results?	
What kind of system can you develop to stay on track, be organized, and deliver results?	
What key performance indicators (KPIs) are used to drive performance in your area?	
How can your mentor support you?	
How will you know you are improving in this area?	

Coach/Mentor Questions

Questions	Responses
How have you educated yourself to be culturally sensitive?	
How have you learned about other cultures, backgrounds, and generations?	
How are you continuing to improve your cross-cultural communication skills?	
What did you learn about yourself from your self-assessment?	
What are some things you do to drive your performance?	
What are the benefits of your team driving performance?	
What is one area of improvement for you in terms of driving performance?	
Do you ever have a problem consistently delivering results?	
What kind of system can you develop to stay on track, be organized, and deliver results?	
What key performance indicators (KPIs) can we use to drive performance?	
How will you know you are improving in this area?	
How can I support you?	
Assignment for Next Week:	

> *"And what is a man without energy? Nothing—nothing at all."*
> —Mark Twain

Working in food service requires a lot of energy and strategies for self-care. It's essential to take care of yourself to maintain high energy levels and improve your self-care skills.

Do you possess energy that draws people to you, or do you bring down the group because of your lack of energy? Think about people in your life to whom you are attracted because of their energy. How do you come across?

How can you change this if your energy level is low? Are you taking care of yourself? Do you exercise? Do you eat healthy foods? Do you drink enough water? Do you get enough sleep? Do you think this is crucial?

Start taking better care of yourself. Working in food service takes great energy; in this business, people skip taking care of themselves because they are taking care of others. Plan your meals so you can better maintain a healthy lifestyle. Drink water throughout the day. Stop drinking sugary drinks or souped-up energy drinks; they do not help energy levels. If you start to feel your energy subsiding, breathe.

Do you surround yourself with positive and forward-thinking people? Do you take vacations to rejuvenate? Do you carve out downtime to recapture your creativity? Do you keep yourself inspired with quotes, books, and affirmations? Do you have a hobby you are enthusiastic about that fulfills you? Do you approach life as the glass is half empty rather than half full and think this is all there is to life? Are you resilient at work? Do you feel loved in your relationships? Do you have a spiritual practice that uplifts you? What are you passionate about? What do you want out of life? Do you know your life's purpose? What are the possibilities in your life? What goals and actions have you put in place?

Once you tap into answering these questions, your energy level will improve. Think about a time when your energy was high. You could do and tackle anything; you were in the zone. What caused the elevated level of energy? What were you doing at the time that made you feel energized? Consider the possibility that you were acting on things important to you.

Finally, get enough sleep to tackle the next day with the energy level that serves you best. Too many people are sleep-deprived, which is a real problem. According to Larry Alton (2016), a professional blogger and researcher, there is a relationship between sleep and worker productivity. We all need and want more sleep but cannot always get a quality night's sleep. Pay attention to what works for you. Give yourself permission to go to bed earlier to enjoy eight hours of sleep. Ensure you turn off all electronic devices at least an hour before bed to reduce stimulation. Ensure you have a good mattress, a dark room, and the right room temperature. These should help give you the energy to tackle your day ahead. If you are a person who wakes up in the middle of the night consumed by thoughts, have a journal and pen by your bed. Write the thoughts down and go back to sleep. You can train your brain to know there is a system for capturing thoughts; this can settle your mind so you can go back to sleep. Journaling is more effective than lying in bed, thinking, not being able to sleep, and then getting up in the morning more tired than when you went to bed the night before.

Focusing on these areas can boost your energy levels, improve your self-care skills, and prepare for a successful reentry into society. Remember, you are worth it!

Self-Assessment Questions

How would you rate your energy level on a scale of one to ten, with one being poor and ten being excellent?	
What personal energy areas could you improve? _____Healthy eating _____Exercise daily _____Drinking more water _____Sleeping at least eight hours a night _____Relationships _____Setting goals	
What is an area of interest to start on first?	
What actions will you take?	
How will you know you are making progress?	

Coach/Mentor Questions

Describe your personal energy level at this point in your life.	
How can you improve your energy level based on your personal assessment?	
In what area will you start? _____ Healthy eating _____ Exercise daily _____ Drinking more water _____ Sleeping at least eight hours a night _____ Relationships _____ Setting goals	
Do you surround yourself with positive people who add to your life? If there is anyone who is toxic to you, what will you do about it?	
What are you passionate about? What goals have you set for yourself?	
What do you want your life to stand for?	
What do you want in your life?	
How will you measure your improvement in this area?	
How can I support you?	
Assignment for Next Week:	

F IS FOR FOODSERVICE

> *"Before anything else, preparation is the key to success."*
> —Alexander Graham Bell

Foodservice is one of the most fascinating industries to work in today. This is the right industry for you if you love serving people and get joy when someone compliments your food or comments on your smile. It is a potential career path with a lifetime of growth opportunities. Career possibilities include fast food, healthcare, fine dining, country clubs, cruise ships, catering, event management, and more.

When our customers, patients, or seniors come to us and eat our food, they trust us with their lives. You might not have thought about how vital your role is to our operation.

Nutrition is an integral part of daily life. For our seniors, it is for their health and well-being. It is a source of energy for our employees and residents. Food creates a sense of bonding. For some of us, food is a source of comfort during stressful times. For families, it is at the center of celebrations and traditions. A smile is equally significant.

Foodservice is also a serious industry in which we are held responsible by specific accreditation standards and state and local health department standards. Here are some standards you must be aware of to maintain compliance:

Food Liabilities

Employee Hygiene

Have you ever thought about how significant your role is in food and nutrition services? Did you know we are accountable to the public by upholding health or accreditation standards? Do you know how comprehensive they are and what happens when we do not comply?

Do you ever think about the legalities for which you are personally accountable every time you are at work?

Our daily PPE includes gloves, hand washing, hair nets, beard guards, aprons, and covering open sores and cuts when handling food. We must also be self-aware, not touch our faces or hair during our shift, and wash our hands between glove changes.

In addition, we must ensure our workspaces are clean and sanitized, including cutting boards and equipment. We also must think about how to handle cups, glasses, and silverware by the handles and much more.

Safety

What are the reasons we practice safe handling of leftover foods? What are the proper temperatures for freezing, thawing, preparation, holding, and serving?

Are you knowledgeable about maintaining a safe work environment, such as flooring and walkways, and how to report accidents? Do you know the fire evacuation process?

Abuse and Resident Rights

When our residents and staff are part of our operation, do you think they feel our team cares, gets along, and supports one another? What is the feel of the organization/team? When staff and visitors are touring the kitchen, what perceptions do they have about our operation? Do you respect and appreciate the individual differences between our workforce and our customer population? Do you speak respectfully and politely in every interaction? Do you take initiative at work and take on the responsibility by interacting with coworkers and staff? Do you treat everyone with respect?

Compliance and Ethics

What is your organization's mission statement? Can you repeat it? How do you think food service and nutrition impact the mission? Are you knowledgeable about compliance and ethics expectations and standards?

Menus and Nutritional Adequacy

Are you ensuring we deliver the right food to residents and staff and follow dietary requirements or cultural choices? Are you using portion control? Do you know what you can modify in meals for customers whose special needs restrict their diets or allergies? How knowledgeable are you about the ingredients in each menu item? Can you imagine what might happen if you served a menu item the person was allergic to? Do you know what happens when someone is allergic to peanuts and accidentally ingests a food item containing peanuts?

Did you know that about thirty-two million people in the United States have food allergies? Does that surprise you? Do you have food allergies, or are you familiar with the most common allergies?

Here is a scenario to consider: Suppose you were entertaining at home and invited guests to dinner. As a matter of practice, would you ask them if there are any foods, spices, or herbs they are allergic to? These are things to start thinking about with family members or working in a commercial kitchen post-release.

Self-Assessment Questions

Questions	Responses
What are some things you know that are essential for hand hygiene? What steps do you take when working? What mistakes do you think we sometimes make?	
What is our PPE in food service and nutrition?	
What steps do you take to maintain safety at work? List some examples of potential safety hazards to look out for.	
Does your team care, get along, and support one another? What do you do to contribute to the unit's feel?	
When our residents or staff receive the food we create, how does it make them feel?	
How do you think our food service and nutrition department impacts your organization's mission?	
Are you ensuring we cook and deliver the right food to the right residents or staff, following the dietary requirements and cultural choices?	
What are the proper temperatures to pay attention to ensure food safety?	
What can we modify in meals for residents whose special needs restrict their diets?	

How knowledgeable are you with the ingredients in each menu item? What do you want to learn?	
What are some types of food allergies?	
Regarding health department rules or accreditation standards, on a scale of one to ten, with one being I do not know and ten being I can teach it, how comfortable are you with knowing the standards by which we are held accountable?	
What is one area you would like to learn more about?	
What action steps can you take to improve in one of these areas?	
How will you know you are making progress?	

Coach/Mentor Questions

Questions	Responses
What are some things you know are important for hand hygiene? List the steps you take when working. What mistakes do you think we sometimes make?	
What is our PPE in food service and nutrition?	
What steps do you take to maintain safety at work? List some examples of potential safety hazards to look out for.	
Does your team care, get along, and support one another? What do you do to contribute to the unit's feel?	
When our residents or staff receive the food we create, how does it make them feel?	
How do you think our food service and nutrition department impacts our organization's mission?	
Are you ensuring you cook and deliver the right food to the residents and staff, following the dietary requirements and cultural choices?	
What are the proper temperatures to pay attention to ensure food safety?	
What can you modify in meals for residents and staff whose special needs restrict their diets?	

What are some types of food allergies?	
Regarding health department rules or accreditation standards, on a scale of one to ten, with one being I do not know and ten being I can teach it, how comfortable are you with knowing the standards by which we are held accountable?	
What is one area you would like to learn more about?	
What action steps can you take to improve in one of these areas?	
How will you know you are making progress?	
How can I support you?	
Assignment for Next Week:	

> *"Gratitude makes sense of our past, brings peace for today, and creates a vision for tomorrow."*
> —Melody Beattie

Gratitude is being thankful. How many times each day do we miss the opportunity to be grateful? Did you know that practicing gratitude can make your life more meaningful and change your perspective?

Set aside time each day and start by being grateful for at least three things in your life. Either say them aloud or write them down. Keeping a gratitude journal by your bed is extremely helpful for starting and continuing this practice. Putting pen to paper is a powerful tool that activates your brain and senses.

We often fail to acknowledge the small things we are blessed to have or that happen in our lives. Many people focus on what is wrong. If you take the opposite approach and look for things for which to be grateful, you will find more blessings. Bring in all your senses as you write or state the things for which you are grateful. How does it make you feel? What do you see? What do you hear? What about your sense of touch?

So, what does expressing gratitude have to do with promotability? Everything. When you are in business, there are a series of problems to solve, which cause stress. According to Robert Emmons (2004), a world's leading gratitude expert and psychology professor at the University of California Davis, "Gratitude can be that stress buster." It allows you to generate optimism while building strength to recover more quickly from setbacks. Let people in your life know you are grateful for them. Appreciate your coworkers for their contributions.

Lindsay Holmes (2017), the deputy editor for the Huffington Post, says more gratitude equals a better life. That means a better life at home and work. You will feel grateful if you build this habit for over thirty days. Your whole outlook on life will be improved. Pass it on!

For further inspiration, read the "Gratitude Poem" by Nancy J. Carmody and share it with your team. It will reset your perspective. In addition, watch the YouTube video by Warhawk Matt Scott, "No Excuses" https://www.youtube.com/watch?v=obdd31Q9PqA.

Self-Assessment Questions

Do you keep a gratitude journal?	
Would you be willing to write what you are grateful for each morning?	
What did you think of the "Gratitude Poem" and the YouTube video? How did they change your perspective?	
In what areas of your life have you taken people or situations for granted?	
What is one action step you can take today regarding gratitude?	
How will you know you are making progress?	

Coach/Mentor Questions

What did you think of the "Gratitude Poem" and the YouTube video? How did they change your perspective?	
What are you grateful for at work?	
What are you grateful for at home?	
What are you grateful for from your work team?	
What are you grateful for in your relationships?	
What daily practice are you willing to start to keep gratitude at the forefront?	
Is there any area of your life or a person you have taken for granted?	
How will you measure your improvement in this area?	
How can I support you?	
Assignment for Next Week:	

I Am Thankful For by Nancy J Carmody (2002)

I am thankful for

…the mess to clean up after a party

because it means I have been surrounded by friends.

…the taxes that I pay

because it means that I'm employed.

…the clothes that fit a little too snug

because it means I have enough to eat.

…my shadow who watches me work

because it means I am out in the sunshine.

…the spot I find at the far end of the parking lot

because it means I am capable of walking.

…all the complaining I hear about our government

because it means we have freedom of speech.

…that lady behind me in church who sings off key

because it means that I can hear.

…lawn that needs mowing, windows that need cleaning, and gutters that need fixing

because it means I have a home.

…my huge heating bill

because it means that I am warm.

…weariness and aching muscles at the end of the day

because it means that I have been productive.

…the alarm that goes off in the early morning hours

because it means that I am alive.

> *"We are what we repeatedly do. Excellence, then,*
> *is not an act but a habit."*
> —Aristotle

Hospitality is the friendly and generous reception and entertainment of guests, visitors, or strangers. How do you provide excellent customer service in your role? With your colleagues? With your managers?

We now have an intersection of hospitality and healthcare as we adapt to changing circumstances. There is an increased focus on diversity and inclusion, resident and staff satisfaction, and working to meet new performance criteria. Additionally, we must consider family members' input and that of patients or seniors. All the changes require staff development, leadership training, dealing with older facilities, disaster plans, PPE, technology, and COVID-19 outbreaks. When that is all said and done, today, people want to work with purpose and know that what they do matters.

One of the first lessons to learn in hospitality is to come to work as if you were in charge. For example, look up and down at the floor when you first walk in. Look to see if any lights are out and need replacement. Turn in a service request. Look on the floor to see if you need to pick up paper or trash, if a spill needs mopping, or if a wet floor sign is needed. Walk in each day as if it is your first day on the job and take ownership. Then, look at each station. Is each area clean? Can you help? Where are opportunities for improvement?

Stand where our residents or customers stand and think about what they see. Are we putting our best foot forward? Do our customers feel we are a great team? Do they feel welcome? Are we proud of the food we serve? Do we call our customers by name? Do we welcome them by saying, "Good morning" or "Good afternoon"?

If you were the general manager for the day, what is one area you would focus on to improve our service or operation?

Self-Assessment Questions

How do you provide excellent customer service?	
What are some changing circumstances you've noticed in the food service industry?	
What are some of your ideas for operational improvement?	
If you were the general manager for the day, what is one area you would focus on to improve our service or operation?	

Coach/Mentor Questions

How do you provide excellent customer service?	
When you think about the food service industry, what changes have you noticed?	
What are some of your ideas for operational improvement?	
If you were the general manager for the day, what is one area you would focus on to improve our service or operation?	
How can I support you?	
Assignment for Next Week:	

> *"A single lie destroys a whole reputation of integrity."*
> —Baltasar Gracian

Integrity is always doing what you say, regardless of whether anyone is watching you or knows. It is the state of being in integrity with yourself—keeping and honoring your word and promises to yourself and your friends, family, and coworkers. You will be amazed at how free you feel when you know that you can keep your word and others can count on you. However, integrity doesn't mean always saying yes.

Here is a situation to consider: Are you great at work about keeping your word, but when it comes to yourself, not so much—or vice versa? Take an honest look at your life and decide where you can improve your integrity muscle. It will take practice, but you grow each day you try. To make this trait real, you need to dig deep and tell the truth to yourself.

Here are some areas to think about: Do you gossip about others? Have you taken things without paying for them? Have you taken office supplies home for personal use? Have you used the company copier to copy personal things? Do you tell little white lies and justify them? Do you play fast and loose with the truth? Have you exceeded the speed limit in the past? Have you ever parked in a handicapped accessible parking space, even though you are not handicapped? Do you think the rules do not apply to you? Have you hurt some-one's feelings and never apologized? Have you been charged less for an item at a store and failed to tell them they charged you the wrong amount? Have you ever found money on the floor at a store and failed to turn it in? Have you disclosed confidential information about your company or a project? Have you used work time on social media when you were supposed to be working? Have you ever made a mistake at work and failed to own it? Did you fail to meet a company deadline? Do you follow company policies 100 percent of the time? Have you taken credit for someone else's work? Have you ever compromised your values? Do you have the courage to tell the truth? Have you committed a crime and not dealt with the consequences of the people you hurt?

Or you are great at keeping your word with others but not when it comes to yourself. Do you have integrity in yourself? Do you keep your word to yourself? For example, do you tell yourself you will go to the gym three days a week and not follow through? Do you tell yourself that you want to seek an opportunity to be promoted but not share this goal with your manager or take the necessary steps to be ready to apply?

Look for opportunities to improve each day in this area. How can you build your integrity muscle?

Be honest. When you make a mistake, own it. Be a person of your word. Become someone everyone can count on, no matter what. Know that you can rely on yourself. Know that you are your word. The more you practice the integrity muscle, the stronger you become. It is just like working out. You know you have arrived when you can count on your word and yourself. Integrity is a crucial characteristic of leadership.

Good luck getting stronger every day!

Self-Assessment Questions

What does integrity mean to you?	
Is integrity important in a leadership role?	
When you read the examples, did you see yourself in any of them?	
Whom do you admire because of their integrity? What company displays integrity?	
What examples of leaders who have failed to have integrity in business can you think of? What happened? If you're not aware of any, research and share.	
What is one area you can work on for yourself?	
How do you justify your behavior when your integrity is not intact?	
How will you know you are making progress?	
How will you know when you can keep your word? To yourself? To others?	

Coach/Mentor Questions

What does integrity mean to you?	
What did you think of some of the examples provided? Let's discuss a few.	
Have you ever looked at integrity in this way? What surprised you?	
If you were in a leadership position, how would you model integrity?	
In your current position, how do you demonstrate integrity?	
What happens when a leader does not model integrity? What happens to the organization? To the culture? To the people? Can you give some specific examples?	
How will you measure your improvement in this area?	
How can I support you?	
Assignment for Next Week:	

J IS FOR JADED

> *"I suppose there are many reasons to be jaded or sarcastic, but I hang onto the reasons why life is beautiful."*
> —Kellie O'Hara

Are you jaded because of world events? Are you feeling cynical about life? Do you feel disappointed by athletes and people in the media? Do you think life is not fair and you have been passed over? Do you complain about *those* people at work? Are you the person sitting in the stands and yelling but doing nothing, or do you see a situation and want to become an agent of change? Do you complain about your situation, peers, or leadership? Or do you take the high road? Do you get involved in your community to improve the quality of life? Do you engage others to join you? Who are you in these scenarios? Are you in the stands or on the field?

According to the Merriam-Webster Dictionary, jaded is feeling "dull or cynical." Do you feel entitled to be cynical because you have been wronged at work? Do you feel like people at work are not doing their part? Did you know that being pessimistic is a defensive posture to try to protect yourself? However, being cynical can dramatically decrease the quality and health of your life. When you see the world from this perspective, everything is dull, and there is no joy. The only person suffering is you. So, if there is an opportunity for a promotion at your workplace, what reason would leadership have to promote someone cynical? I cannot think of any, can you?

If you want to take the path to have the possibility of being promoted, you can take a different approach and improve the quality of your life. You can take the high road, become a change agent, and become more positive. You can become compassionate toward others. Instead of looking for what is wrong in every situation, begin looking for what is right. Decide who you want to be. Your future is in your hands!

Self-Assessment Questions

On a scale of one to ten, with one being feeling jaded all the time and ten being never feeling jaded, how would you rate yourself?	
In what areas do you struggle with cynicism (believe people are generously selfish and dishonest)?	
How can you change this outlook?	
How will you know you are starting to shift your perspective?	

Coach/Mentor Questions

Are there areas at work where you feel jaded? What happened?	
What is the root cause?	
How can you change your perspective?	
How would you coach someone who is jaded? How can you propose an alternative perspective?	
What strategies might work to improve the situation?	
What resources might be available?	
How can I support you?	
Assignment for Next Week:	

K IS FOR KNOWLEDGE

> *"Who looks outside, dreams. Who looks inside, awakens."*
> —Carl Jung

What are some of the traits and skills necessary for success in the food service industry?

- Are you friendly, outgoing, and people-oriented?
- Are you energetic and creative?
- Are you okay with working long hours?
- Do you have a good customer service attitude?
- Do you like to learn new things?

Have you ever considered becoming a sous chef, executive chef, food service manager, or owner-operator? What would it take to get there?

How well do you know all aspects of your role in the company? How well do you know the entire organization's operations? What do you need to know? What skills do you need that you may be lacking? Are there certifications or education that would enhance your promotability? Decide what you want to learn. Do you want to go wide or deep? Do you want to specialize in an area? Develop a plan to gain the knowledge you need to fill the gaps.

Knowledge is defined as facts, information, and skills you learn through education and experience. How can you increase your knowledge? You can read. You can ask questions. You can seek a mentor or business coach. Is there training available to enhance your skill set, either inside or outside the company? Is there a professional organization you could join?

Food Allergies

What is a food allergy? It is defined as a medical condition in which exposure to food triggers a harmful immune response. Food allergies are a growing public health and food safety concern affecting an estimated twenty-six million people in the US. Eight foods are responsible for 90 percent of all food allergic reactions in the US. They are milk, eggs, fish, shellfish, wheat, tree nuts, peanuts, and soybeans, updated by the CDC Environmental Health Specialists and conducted by an EHS-Net study (2022).

A vital part of the food service industry is knowing that cross-contamination can occur when food touches surfaces, utensils, and equipment, as they can carry the slightest traces of the allergen. Cross-contamination can lead to foodborne illness from bacteria and viruses because of improper preparation and storage temperature.

A serious part of our industry is being mindful of people and food allergies. Did you know that if a customer has a food allergy, consuming only a small amount can have damaging effects? People can experience trouble breathing and cramping and can develop hives, swollen tongues, and throats. Food allergies can even result in anaphylactic shock and lead to death. Do you know anyone who has a food allergy? If yes, what are they allergic to, and what happens when they come into contact with that food?

Do you know how to respond to a food allergy emergency?

Self-Assessment Questions

Questions	Responses
Where do you see your career in food service going? What are your long-term career goals?	
What certification, training, or education do you need to progress in your career?	
What did you learn from this section that you did not know?	
How knowledgeable are you about food allergies?	
What area do you need to learn more about in terms of the industry or food allergies?	
What is one action step you can take to improve in this area?	
How will you know you are making progress?	

Coach/Mentor Questions

Questions	Responses
Where do you see your career in food service going? What are your long-term career goals?	
What certification, training, or education do you need to progress in your career?	
What did you learn from this section that you did not know?	
How knowledgeable are you about food allergies?	
What area do you need to learn more about in terms of the industry or food allergies?	
What is one action step you can take to improve in this area?	
How will you know you are making progress?	
How can you all support each other?	
How can I support you?	
Assignment for Next Week:	

> *"Life is not about finding yourself.*
> *Life is about creating yourself."*
> —George Bernard Shaw

Do you love to learn? Do you have a passion for trying new things? Do you engage in learning new things both inside and outside of work? Do you look for ways to stretch your creative capacity and yourself? I often feel like a kid in the candy store when it comes to learning. I feel like there is not enough time to learn about everything I am interested in, but in a good and invigorating way. I make the time because it changes me. It opens my mind to new possibilities. I use what I learn from new areas to bring back to work in my role and apply it. I learn from others and broaden my perspective. I take personal development courses to uncover my bias or understand my thinking more effectively.

Learning doesn't have to be formal. I take every opportunity to learn something new. Here is an example you might consider, as you have no idea where a career in food service can take you.

Dining Room Etiquette: A Guide for Inmates Working in the Prison Kitchen

Working in the prison kitchen offers a unique opportunity to learn valuable skills that can be applied in the food service industry upon release. Understanding dining room etiquette is crucial, especially if you aspire to move into management roles where knowledge of both front and back-of-the-house operations is essential. Here's a guide to help you master dining room etiquette and use it as a steppingstone for lifelong learning and career growth.

Understanding Dining Room Etiquette

Dining room etiquette encompasses the standards and practices that ensure a pleasant dining experience for guests. Here are some key aspects:

- Greeting Guests: Always greet guests with a warm smile and polite greeting. This sets a positive tone for their dining experience.

- Proper Attire: Wear a clean and appropriate uniform. Personal hygiene is crucial in maintaining a professional appearance.
- Table Setting: Learn the correct way to set a table, including the placement of utensils, plates, and glasses. This attention to detail reflects the quality of service.
- Serving Food and Beverages: Serve from the left and clear from the right. Be attentive to guests' needs without being intrusive.
- Handling Complaints: Address complaints calmly and professionally. Listen to the guest, apologize for any inconvenience, and take appropriate action to resolve the issue.

Setting a Table American Style

Setting a table American style involves specific placement of utensils, plates, and glasses. Here's a step-by-step guide with diagrams.

1. **Basic Table Setting**:

   o Dinner Plate: Place the dinner plate in the center.
   o Forks: Place the fork to the left of the plate.
   o Knife and Spoon: Place the knife to the right of the plate with the blade facing the plate and the spoon to the right of the knife.
   o Glassware: Place the water glass above the knife.

2. **Casual Table Setting**:

    o Salad Plate: Place the salad plate on top of the dinner plate.
    o Forks: Place the salad fork to the left of the dinner fork.
    o Knife and Spoon: Same as the basic setting.
    o Glassware: Add a wine glass to the right of the water glass.

3. **Formal Table Setting**:

    o Charger Plate: Place a charger plate under the dinner plate.
    o Soup Bowl: Place the soup bowl on top of the salad plate.
    o Utensils: Add a soup spoon to the right of the knife and a dessert spoon above the plate.
    o Glassware: Include a water glass, red wine glass, and white wine glass.

Applying These Skills in the Prison Kitchen

While working in the prison kitchen, you can practice these skills daily:

* Teamwork: Collaborate with your fellow inmates to ensure smooth kitchen operations. Effective communication and cooperation are key.

- Attention to Detail: Focus on the quality and presentation of the food you prepare. This habit will serve you well in any food service role.
- Customer Service: Even in a prison setting, providing excellent service to staff and fellow inmates can help you develop strong customer service skills.

Lifelong Learning and Career Advancement

The skills you learn in the prison kitchen can be a foundation for a successful food service career. Here's how you can use this experience to your advantage:

- Resume Building: Highlight your experience in the prison kitchen on your resume. Emphasize your knowledge of dining room etiquette, teamwork, and customer service.
- Further Education: Consider pursuing additional training or certifications in food service management. Many community colleges and vocational schools offer programs that can enhance your skills.
- Networking: Build connections with professionals in the food service industry. Attend job fairs, join industry restaurant, hotel, and/or hospitality associations, and seek mentorship opportunities.

Front and Back of the House Operations

Understanding both front and back of the house operations is crucial for a management role:

- Front of the House: This includes all areas where guests interact with staff, such as the dining room, bar, and reception. Skills in customer service, communication, and dining room etiquette are essential here.
- Back of the House: This includes the kitchen, storage, and administrative areas. Skills in food preparation, inventory management, and kitchen safety are crucial.

By mastering both areas, you'll be well-prepared to take on leadership roles in the food service industry.

Working in the prison kitchen is more than just a job; it's an opportunity to develop valuable skills that can lead to a rewarding career in the food service industry. By understanding and practicing dining room etiquette, you can set yourself up for success and demonstrate your commitment to lifelong learning and professional growth. Remember, every skill you acquire brings you one step closer to achieving your career goals. One critical skill in the food service industry is customer service.

If you like reading, there is an excellent resource by John R. DiJulius III (2003): Secret Service: Hidden Systems that Deliver Unforgettable Customer Service. This book shows you a variety of companies and the systems they use to offer exceptional customer service. As I mentioned before, you can learn a lot by studying all types of companies.

Do you enjoy listening to webinars or podcasts? I love TED talks on YouTube. If you are not familiar with TED, check it out. TED stands for technology, entertainment, and design. These are approximately eighteen-minute video talks by thought leaders who present high-quality information on trending topics. Check out TED on topics that interest you and can help your career.

Do you belong to professional associations or organizations? Are you learning a new language, or do you spend three to four hours a day on social media thinking you are learning new things to enhance your career and promotion possibilities? Expand yourself. Do something different. Make a point to learn something new every day.

Self-Assessment Questions

Rate yourself on a scale of one to ten, with one being I do not care to learn and ten being I have a passion for learning.	
What types of topics interest you?	
What did you learn about dining room operations from the article?	
Have you heard of or watched TED talks on YouTube? What are three of your favorites?	
What was the last book you read or listened to?	
What podcasts do you listen to?	
Do you speak more than one language?	
What lessons can you learn from other industries? How can you learn them?	
What good and poor customer service examples can you provide?	
How can you encourage others to be lifelong learners?	

Coach/Mentor Questions

How did you rate yourself on the topic of being a lifelong learner? Explain.	
What areas of learning do you enjoy?	
What did you learn about dining room operations that you never realized?	
What was the last book you read or listened to?	
What podcasts do you listen to?	
Do you speak more than one language?	
What have you done to develop your creativity?	
How can you encourage others to be lifelong learners?	
Give me an example of excellent customer service you have noticed.	
Give me one example of poor customer service you received.	
How can we share opportunities for growth in this area?	
How can I support you?	
Assignment for Next Week:	

M IS FOR MINDSET

Do you have a fixed mindset or a growth mindset? How do you know? When you make a mistake, do you think you should stop or quit because you failed? Do you avoid risk and challenges? When you are learning something new, and it is challenging and does not come quickly, what is your self-talk? Do you say, "It is something new to learn"? Do you want to be praised for the effort and journey?

Mindset is defined as a set of attitudes one possesses. One of the best resources about mindset is Carol S. Dweck's book *Mindset: The New Psychology of Success: How We Can Learn to Fulfill Our Potential.* Read it or Google it and see how you can develop a growth mindset in all areas of your life. Dr. Carol S. Dweck describes a fixed mindset as static, avoids challenges, sees the effort as fruitless, ignores useful negative feedback, and feels threatened by the success of others. She then describes the characteristics of a growth mindset. Those with a growth mindset have the desire to learn, embrace challenges, are persistent, learn from criticism, and are inspired by others. Who are you?

Let's test your mindset with a riddle.

> *Bobby and his father are in a horrible car accident, which instantly kills his father. Bobby is seriously injured and rushed to the hospital. The surgeon takes one look at Bobby on the operating table and says, "Oh my God! I can't operate on this boy. He is my son!"*

How can this be? What is the point of this riddle? The answer thirty years ago was that the surgeon was his mother. Today, the answer could also be his other father.

Applying Growth Mindset in the Prison Kitchen: Scenarios and Strategies

Carol S. Dweck's research on mindsets highlights the importance of adopting a growth mindset to achieve personal and professional success. Here are some scenarios that illustrate the difference between a growth mindset and a fixed mindset for inmates working in a prison kitchen, along with strategies to overcome a fixed mindset.

1. **Scenario: Learning a New Recipe**

   - Fixed Mindset: "I can't learn this new recipe. I'm just not good at cooking."
   - Growth Mindset: "I may not know this recipe yet, but with practice, I can learn it and improve my cooking skills."

   Strategy to Overcome Fixed Mindset:

   - What to Say: "It's okay to make mistakes while learning. Each attempt is a step toward mastering the recipe. Let's break it down into smaller steps and tackle it one part at a time."

2. **Scenario: Handling Criticism**

   - Fixed Mindset: "The supervisor said my dish wasn't good enough. I'm just not cut out for this."
   - Growth Mindset: "The supervisor's feedback is an opportunity for me to improve. I can use their suggestions to make my dish better next time."

   Strategy to Overcome Fixed Mindset:

   - What to Say: "Feedback is a tool for growth. Let's focus on what we can learn from it and how we can apply it to improve our skills."

3. **Scenario: Working Under Pressure**

   - Fixed Mindset: "This is too stressful. I can't handle the pressure of working in the kitchen."
   - Growth Mindset: "Working under pressure is challenging, but it's also a chance to develop my time-management and problem-solving skills."

   Strategy to Overcome Fixed Mindset:

   - What to Say: "Stressful situations are part of the learning process. Let's take a deep breath, prioritize our tasks, and tackle them one by one."

4. **Scenario: Collaborating with Others**

- Fixed Mindset: "I don't get along with my teammates. It's impossible to work with them."
- Growth Mindset: "Building good relationships with my teammates takes effort, but it's essential for a smooth kitchen operation. I can learn to communicate better and work collaboratively."

Strategy to Overcome Fixed Mindset:

- What to Say: "Teamwork is key to success in the kitchen. Let's find ways to improve our communication and support each other."

Strategies for Developing a Growth Mindset

1. Embrace Challenges: View challenges as opportunities to learn and grow. Remind yourself that every difficult task is a chance to develop new skills.

2. Learn from Criticism: Accept feedback as a valuable resource for improvement. Focus on the constructive aspects of criticism and use it to enhance your abilities.

3. Celebrate Effort: Recognize and celebrate the effort you put into your work, regardless of the outcome. Effort is the path to mastery.

4. Persist Through Setbacks: Understand that setbacks are a natural part of the learning process. Use them as motivation to keep trying and improving.

5. Cultivate Curiosity: Stay curious and open to learning new things. Ask questions, seek new knowledge, and be willing to experiment.

Adopting a growth mindset can transform your experience in the prison kitchen and beyond. By viewing challenges as opportunities, learning from feedback, and persisting through setbacks, you can develop valuable skills that will serve you well in any career. Remember, the journey is a continuous process of learning and growth.

Practicing growth mindset strategies daily can help inmates working in the prison kitchen develop resilience and adaptability. Here are some practical ways to incorporate these strategies into your daily routine:

Embrace Challenges

- Daily Practice: Take on a new task or recipe each day, even if it seems difficult. Approach it with curiosity and a willingness to learn.
- Example: If there's a complex dish on the menu, volunteer to help prepare it. Use it as an opportunity to learn new techniques.

Learn from Criticism

- Daily Practice: Seek feedback from supervisors and peers regularly. Reflect on the feedback and identify specific areas for improvement.
- Example: After each shift, ask for constructive feedback on your performance. Write down the suggestions and make a plan to work on them.

Celebrate Effort

- Daily Practice: Acknowledge your efforts and progress, no matter how small. Keep a journal to track your achievements and the hard work you put in.
- Example: At the end of each day, write down one thing you did well and one thing you learned. Celebrate the effort you made to improve.

Persist Through Setbacks

- Daily Practice: When faced with a setback, take a moment to reflect on what went wrong and how you can approach it differently next time.
- Example: If a dish doesn't turn out as expected, analyze what went wrong and try again. Use each attempt as a learning experience.

Cultivate Curiosity

- Daily Practice: Ask questions and seek new knowledge. Be open to learning from everyone around you, including your peers.
- Example: If you see someone using an unfamiliar technique, ask them to explain it to you. Show interest in learning new skills.

Daily Reflection and Goal Setting

- Daily Practice: Spend a few minutes each day reflecting on your experiences and setting goals for the next day. This helps reinforce a growth mindset.
- Example: At the end of each shift, reflect on what you learned and set a specific goal for the next day, such as mastering a new recipe or improving your teamwork skills.

Positive Self-Talk

- Daily Practice: Use positive affirmations and self-talk to reinforce a growth mindset. Remind yourself that you are capable of learning and growing.
- Example: Start your day with affirmations like, "I am capable of learning new skills," or "Every challenge is an opportunity to grow."

Peer Support

- Daily Practice: Support and encourage your peers to adopt a growth mindset. Share your experiences and strategies with them.
- Example: Form a study group with fellow inmates to discuss challenges and share tips on overcoming them. Encourage each other to keep pushing forward.

By incorporating these strategies into your daily routine, you can develop a strong growth mindset that will serve you well in the kitchen and beyond. This mindset will help you face challenges with confidence, learn from your experiences, and continuously strive for improvement. Now, let's start challenging your thinking.

Self-Assessment Questions

Overall, do you feel you have a growth or a fixed mindset?	
In what areas of your life do you have a growth mindset?	
In what areas of your life do you have a fixed mindset? What are some limiting beliefs that block your potential?	
Can you share an example of a time when you received feedback in the kitchen? How did you respond to it, and what did you learn from the experience?	
What do you say to yourself when things are hard or when you're learning something for the first time?	
What is one challenging task or recipe you have taken on recently? How did you approach it, and what strategies did you use to overcome difficulties?	
How have you practiced the growth mindset strategies in your daily routine? Can you describe a specific instance where you applied these strategies and the outcome?	
How can you measure your growth in this area?	

Coach/Mentor Questions

Describe a growth mindset.	
Describe a fixed mindset.	
Do you feel you have a growth mindset or a fixed mindset?	
In what areas of your life do you have a growth mindset?	
In what areas of your life do you have a fixed mindset?	
What do you say to yourself when things are hard or when you're learning something for the first time?	
What is one challenging task or recipe you have taken on recently? How did you approach it, and what strategies did you use to overcome difficulties?	
How have you practiced the growth mindset strategies in your daily routine? Can you describe a specific instance where you applied these strategies and the outcome?	
How can I encourage your growth in this area?	
We are halfway through the twenty-six traits; what have you learned so far?	
How have you changed?	
How can I support you?	
Assignment for Next Week:	

> *"Words satisfy the soul as food satisfies the stomach; the right words on a person's lips bring satisfaction."*
> —Proverbs 18:20

Nutrition plays a crucial role in maintaining the health and well-being of individuals, especially in a prison environment where access to diverse food options may be limited. Employees who work in the prison kitchen are responsible for ensuring the meals prepared are filling and nutritious. Here are some key points to consider:

1. **Balanced Diet:**

   o Macronutrients: Ensure meals contain a balance of carbohydrates, proteins, and fats. Carbohydrates provide energy, proteins are essential for muscle repair and growth, and fats are necessary for various bodily functions.
   o Micronutrients: Include a variety of fruits and vegetables to provide essential vitamins and minerals. These nutrients are vital for immune function, bone health, and overall well-being.

2. **Food Safety:**

   o Hygiene: Maintain high standards of cleanliness to prevent foodborne illnesses. This includes proper handwashing, sanitizing surfaces, and storing food at the correct temperatures.
   o Preparation: Follow safe food preparation practices, such as cooking meat to the appropriate temperature and avoiding cross-contamination between raw and cooked foods.

3. **Special Dietary Needs:**

   o Allergies and Intolerances: Be aware of inmates' dietary restrictions and ensure meals are prepared to accommodate these needs.

o Medical Diets: Some inmates may require special diets for medical reasons, such as diabetes or hypertension. Providing appropriate meals can help manage these conditions.

4. **Education:**

   o Nutritional Knowledge: Employees should be educated about the basics of nutrition and the importance of a balanced diet. This knowledge can help them make better food choices and prepare healthier meals.
   o Cooking Skills: Training in cooking techniques can improve the meal's quality and nutritional value.

Nutrition Post-Release

After release, maintaining good nutrition is essential for reintegration into society and overall health. Here are some important aspects to consider:

1. **Healthy Eating Habits:**

   o Meal Planning: Plan meals ahead of time to ensure a balanced diet. This can help avoid the temptation of unhealthy fast food and snacks.
   o Portion Control: Be mindful of portion sizes to avoid overeating. Eating smaller, more frequent meals can help maintain energy levels throughout the day.

2. **Access to Healthy Foods:**

   o Grocery Shopping: Learn how to shop for healthy foods on a budget. Focus on purchasing fresh fruits and vegetables, whole grains, lean proteins, and healthy fats.
   o Cooking at Home: Cooking meals at home allows for better control over ingredients and portion sizes. It can also be more cost-effective than eating out.

3. **Continued Education:**

   o Nutritional Literacy: Continue to educate yourself about nutrition. Understanding food labels, nutritional information, and healthy cooking techniques can empower you to make better food choices.
   o Community Resources: Utilize community resources such as food banks, nutrition classes, and support groups to maintain a healthy diet.

4. **Physical and Mental Health:**

   o Exercise: Combine good nutrition with regular physical activity to maintain a healthy weight and improve overall health.

o   Mental Well-being: Good nutrition can positively impact mental health. Eating a balanced diet can help reduce stress, improve mood, and increase energy levels.

What Employees Should Learn

1. **Nutritional Basics:**

   o   Understand the importance of macronutrients and micronutrients.
   o   Learn about the dietary needs of different populations, including those with medical conditions.

2. **Food Safety and Hygiene:**

   o   Master safe food handling and preparation techniques.
   o   Stay updated on food safety regulations and best practices.

3. **Cooking Skills:**

   o   Develop skills in preparing healthy, balanced meals.
   o   Experiment with different cooking methods to retain the nutritional value of foods.

4. **Health and Wellness:**

   o   Recognize the connection between nutrition, physical health, and mental well-being.
   o   Promote healthy eating habits and lifestyle choices among peers and inmates.

By focusing on these areas, employees can contribute to the health and well-being of inmates and prepare themselves for a healthier life post-release. Good nutrition is a cornerstone of overall health, and understanding its importance can lead to better outcomes both inside and outside the prison environment.

Self-Assessment Questions

What is the overall impact of food and nutrition?	
What questions do you have about nutrition?	
What food have you noticed your people enjoy?	
What menu items seem not to be popular or fully consumed?	
Do you pay attention to food trays that come back to the kitchen? What have you noticed?	
How does it make you feel to be concerned about people and their well-being?	

Coach/Mentor Questions

What is the overall impact of food and nutrition?	
What questions do you have about nutrition?	
What food have you noticed your people enjoy?	
What menu items seem not to be popular or fully consumed?	
Do you pay attention to food trays that come back to the kitchen? What have you noticed?	
How does it make you feel to be concerned about people and their well-being?	
How can I support you?	
Assignment for Next Week:	

 IS FOR OPPORTUNITY

Be observant. Look for opportunities to contribute and make a difference. When problems arise, think through how you can bring value instead of complaining.

One of the best examples of this happened when I started my higher education career as a new culinary faculty member. I had taught at this school for three months before the fall session. The culinary department director told me my class in the fall started at 7:00 a.m. So, on the first day of class, I arrived early and set up. At 7:10 a.m., no students were in class. I thought it was strange, so I headed to the Registrar's Office to see the class schedule. The schedule said my class started at 9:00 a.m., not 7:00 a.m. I waited in the faculty and staff lounge until class began. Honestly, it was the best two hours I have ever spent. As each new faculty member came into the lounge, they would ask me where to turn in attendance sheets, how to use the copy machine, where the mailboxes were, about the class schedule and Registrar's Office, etc. I helped every person even though I was new and didn't know everything.

I went to teach my class at 9:00 a.m. The class ended at noon. I promptly went to the Dean of Education's office and asked to speak with him. I had only met him once, and I was nervous. His assistant said he had time to see me. I explained what had occurred to me that morning: Many new teachers were unsure what to do on the first day of class. I told him that in my previous hospitality industry role, we always held a new employee orientation before anyone started. It helped them feel better connected and more confident in the role. He said, "Great idea. You should do that." I laughed to myself, as I had not been given an orientation, but I said, "Yes, I would be happy to do this." I knew I needed to partner with someone at the school who knew the building, the programs, and all the floors. I found that person in Cliff Willson. I asked him if he would help, and he agreed. We held the new-employee orientation every quarter for the next two years. Each time we delivered the orientation, it became better and better.

I could have complained about the situation but chose a different approach. This situation propelled me into some of the most incredible career opportunities in higher education over the next seventeen years.

Think about the problems you see in your kitchen or facility. Reframe problems as opportunities and see where your food service career takes you post-release. In the meantime, keep learning and growing as a professional.

Self-Assessment Questions

What problems or gaps have you noticed in your kitchen or facility that could be viewed as opportunities?	
When have you taken the initiative to bring solutions to your facility? Provide three examples. a. b. c.	
What kind of impact do you want to make?	
How will you know you are making progress?	

Coach/Mentor Questions

Did you learn anything new when you read the example shared as an opportunity?	
What problems or gaps have you noticed in your facility that could be viewed as opportunities?	
When have you taken the initiative to bring solutions to your facility? Provide three examples. a. b. c.	
What kind of impact do you want to make?	
What is one action you can take to improve in this area?	
How will you measure your improvement in this area?	
How can I support you?	
Assignment for Next Week:	

> *"Never bring the problem-solving stage into the decision-making stage. Otherwise, you surrender yourself to the problem rather than the solution."*
> —Robert Schuller

Being known as a great problem solver is a career enhancer. Organizations value employees, managers, and leaders who can solve problems. Since business and technology are moving at such a rapid pace, we must be able to solve problems to grow and develop, both professionally and for the organization.

While many employees may solve problems through trial and error, many other problem-solving models exist. One of my favorite books on the subject was written by Thomas K. Connellan, Ph.D. The book title is *Bringing Out the Best in Others!: 3 Keys for Business Leaders, Educators, Coaches, and Parents*. This is a must-read book for everyone.

My experience, having used and taught the model, is that if you use the three keys together, you can improve performance by 10 to 20 percent. Improvements can be made at work, on your team, and in your family. Reading and applying these three keys is valuable in every aspect of your life: positive expectations, accountability or responsibility, and feedback.

The problem-solving model in *Bringing Out the Best in Others* by Thomas K. Connellan involves several key steps to effectively address and resolve issues. Here is a summary of the model:

1. **Define the Issue:** Clearly state the performance problem without judgment.

2. **Ask for Solutions:** Encourage future-oriented, solution-focused thinking.

3. **Explore Options:** Gather and consider all suggestions without immediate evaluation.

4. **Reinforce Positive Responses:** Turn problems into opportunities for ownership and growth.

Kitchen Scenarios for Problem-Solving

Scenario 1: Food Safety Violation

Issue: During a routine inspection, it was found that raw meat was stored above ready-to-eat foods, posing a risk of cross-contamination.

Steps to Solve:

1. Define the Issue: Clearly state that raw meat was improperly stored, leading to a potential food safety hazard.

2. Ask for Solutions: Ask the kitchen staff for ideas on how to prevent this issue in the future.

3. Explore Options: Consider suggestions such as reorganizing the storage layout, implementing color-coded storage bins, and providing additional training on food safety.

4. Reinforce Positive Responses: Acknowledge and implement the best solutions, and praise the team for their proactive approach to improving food safety.

Scenario 2: Inconsistent Meal Quality

Issue: There have been complaints about the inconsistency in the quality of meals served, with some dishes being overcooked or under-seasoned.

Steps to Solve:

1. Define the Issue: Clearly state that meal quality has been inconsistent, affecting the dining experience.

2. Ask for Solutions: Encourage the kitchen staff to suggest ways to ensure consistent meal quality.

3. Explore Options: Consider suggestions such as standardizing recipes, conducting regular taste tests, and providing additional training on cooking techniques.

4. Reinforce Positive Responses: Implement the best solutions and recognize the team members who contributed valuable ideas.

Scenario 3: Low Employee Morale

Issue: The kitchen staff has been experiencing low morale, leading to decreased productivity and a negative work environment.

Steps to Solve:

1. Define the Issue: Clearly state that low morale is affecting productivity and the work environment.

2. Ask for Solutions: Encourage the staff to share their thoughts on what could improve morale.

3. Explore Options: Consider suggestions such as organizing team-building activities, offering incentives for good performance, and improving communication between management and staff.

4. Reinforce Positive Responses: Implement the best solutions and acknowledge the efforts of the team to create a more positive work environment.

By following this problem-solving model, employees can effectively address and resolve issues in the kitchen, leading to a more efficient and harmonious work environment. Where else can you use this model?

Self-Assessment Questions

When problems arise, how do you solve them?	
Be ready to discuss the three kitchen scenarios and how you can become a better problem solver. a. b. c.	
What problems have you solved at work? Provide three examples.	
How will you know you are making progress in problem-solving?	

Coach/Mentor Questions

When problems arise, how do you solve them?	
Let's discuss the three kitchen scenarios and how you can become a better problem solver. a. b. c.	
What problems have you solved at work? Provide three examples. a. b. c.	
When you solve a problem, do you look at the root cause?	
How do you identify the issue? How do you determine the solution(s)?	
How can you help your team members become better problem solvers?	
How will you know you are making progress in problem-solving?	
How can I support you?	
Assignment for Next Week:	

> *"The art and science of asking questions is the source of all knowledge."*
> —Thomas Berger

The art of asking questions seems to be dwindling due to the fast pace of business. Taking the time to ask questions will save you time and give you the information you need to make informed decisions. Ask questions such as who, what, when, where, and how. Ask clarifying questions so you understand the message intended. Questions inform, provide answers, and show you are interested. Questions are information disguised as power. The more you ask, the more you learn about people, processes, plans, and passion. The more questions you ask, the more interesting you become. It is not in what you know; it is what you learn. If this is an area of weakness for you, learn how to ask essential questions.

There are specific types of questions for particular situations. As far back as Socrates (470–339 BC), the art of asking and answering questions was used to stimulate critical thinking. It helps inform and educate.

Even the Dale Carnegie organization believes that asking questions is an essential people skill. Check out their books and videos online. Asking questions helps inform and build connections with others. What questioning models are you familiar with?

I have spoken with residents, and some can see themselves becoming life coaches. The art of asking questions is a fundamental skill in coaching, enabling coaches to facilitate growth, self-discovery, and problem-solving in their clients. Effective questioning is not just about gathering information; it's about inspiring deeper thinking, uncovering insights, and motivating action. Here's a closer look at the art of questions in coaching, how to become a certified coach, and some questions that kitchen employees can use to grow in their careers. People would rather be asked than told.

In coaching, questions are powerful tools that can transform conversations and lead to significant breakthroughs. Powerful questions are typically open-ended, encouraging clients to explore their thoughts and feelings more deeply. They often begin with "what" or "how," as these prompts invite expansive thinking and reflection. For example, asking, "What would you attempt if you knew you couldn't fail?" can help clients envision new possibilities and overcome self-imposed limitations.

Effective questions in coaching serve several purposes:

- Encourage Self-Discovery: They help clients uncover their values, beliefs, and motivations.
- Stimulate Creative Thinking: They challenge clients to think outside the box and consider new perspectives.
- Promote Action: They motivate clients to take steps toward their goals by clarifying their intentions and plans.

Becoming a Certified Coach

To become a certified coach, one must undergo specific training and meet certain criteria set by recognized coaching organizations. Here are the general steps to becoming a certified coach:

1. **Choose a Coaching Program:**

   o Select a coaching program accredited by a reputable organization, such as the International Coaching Federation (ICF) or Dr. Marshall Goldsmith Stakeholder Centered Coaching (SCC). These programs provide comprehensive training in coaching skills, ethics, and best practices.

2. **Complete Required Training:**

   o Most certification programs require a certain number of training hours. For example, the ICF's Professional Certified Coach (PCC) credential requires 125 hours of coach-specific education.

3. **Gain Coaching Experience:**

   o Accumulate coaching hours by working with clients. The PCC credential requires 500 hours of coaching experience.

4. **Mentor Coaching:**

   o Engage in mentor coaching to receive feedback and guidance from experienced coaches. This helps refine your skills and ensures you are meeting professional standards.

5. **Pass Certification Exams:**

   o Complete performance evaluations and pass written exams to demonstrate your coaching proficiency and knowledge of ethical guidelines.

6. **Continuous Professional Development:**

    o Maintain your certification through ongoing education and professional development to stay current with coaching practices and standards.

Questions for Kitchen Employees to Grow in Their Careers

For kitchen employees looking to advance their careers, asking the right questions can be a powerful tool for personal and professional growth. Here are some questions that can help you reflect on their goals, skills, and development opportunities:

1. **Self-Assessment:**

    o What aspects of my current role do I enjoy the most, and why?
    o What skills have I developed in my current position that I can build upon?

2. **Career Goals:**

    o What are my career goals upon release? What do I not know that I need to know?
    o What steps can I take to achieve these goals?

3. **Skill Development:**

    o What new skills or knowledge do I need to advance in my career?
    o Are there any training programs or certifications that would benefit me now?

4. **Feedback and Improvement:**

    o What feedback have I received from my facility leaders and peers, and how can I use it to improve?
    o What areas do I need to work on to enhance my performance?

5. **Networking and Mentorship:**

    o Who in my network can guide me and support my career development?
    o Are there opportunities for mentorship within my facility?

6. **Work-Life Balance:**

    o How can I manage my time and energy to maintain a healthy work-life balance?
    o What strategies can I implement to reduce stress and prevent burnout?

Regularly reflecting on these questions can clarify your career aspirations, identify areas for improvement, and help you take proactive steps toward professional growth. Effective questioning and a commitment to continuous learning and development can lead to a fulfilling and successful career in the food service industry.

Reduce your talking, ask more questions, and increase your listening capacity. It might keep you from jumping to the wrong conclusions. If you are not listening, you fill in the blanks with your thoughts or meaning, distorting communication outcomes.

How attractive you become to others when you are fully present and listening might surprise you. Think about it. How do you feel when someone really listens to you?

Self-Assessment Questions

How is problem-solving related to asking questions?	
Have you ever thought about the types of questions you ask?	
Do you use a questioning model?	
Research three questioning resources. These can include books, podcasts, or TED talks. Be ready to discuss. a. b. c.	
How will you know you are improving your questioning ability?	

Coach/Mentor Questions

Problem-solving and asking questions are related. Explain to me the relationship and how it can enhance your promotability traits.	
What did you find when you researched three questioning resources? Let's discuss.	
How can you help your team members become better at asking questions rather than jumping to conclusions or voicing their opinions?	
Compare and contrast two people on your team and their questioning abilities.	
Create a plan for continuing to develop your questioning skills.	
How can I support you?	
Assignment for Next Week:	

R IS FOR REVENUE AND RESPONSIBILITY

> *"You cannot escape the responsibility of tomorrow by evading it today."*
> —Abraham Lincoln.

The success of a food service operation depends on many factors that can heavily affect a business's success; some aspects include location, food trends, customer service, and the operations' atmosphere, as well as how good the food is. Many food service operators mess up revenue management, in addition to customer service. Without good customer service, our customers, visitors, and patients will be turned off. While we are not a profit-making operation, our job (everyone's job) is to make sure we break even. Think about it this way: You get a paycheck every two weeks. What does that paycheck have to cover? You want to make sure you can pay your bills and not have a deficit. It would be great to have money at the end of the month. It is the same process in food and nutrition. We have a budget and must cover our costs. While there is no pressure to make a profit, we are still responsible for breaking even. Again, it is everyone's job.

Have you ever thought about what costs we must cover when you see a $3 item? There is the cost to buy the product, and what else? Generate a list of expenses.

Do you know what food and drink items are most popular? Do you know what items are slower-selling items?

How do we know? We have our POS (point of sale) system to tell us. What are some reasons for rotating menu items? Some of the items on the menu we sell are comfort food items. What are some of your favorite comfort foods?

Responsibility is being accountable and taking opportunities to act independently. Being responsible is one way to stand out in front of your boss so you get noticed. What are the actual steps to taking on more responsibility? Alex Cavoulacos, president and founder of *The Muse*, wrote an excellent article titled "5 Ways to Take on More Responsibility at Work." First, let's assume you are good at your current role.

In your next group meeting, talk with your boss about the knowledge and skills you want to develop further. Look for opportunities to help team members. Decide what areas you want to become an expert in, the person everyone in the department goes to because you stay on top of developments and trends.

When developing high-potential employees, we look for the one who takes the initiative, the employee who brings innovative ideas or solutions, and who is proactive rather than waiting to be told what to do next. The employee who waits to be told what to do is marginal. In this fast-paced world, we cannot accept marginal or just doing our job, *especially* if we want to be recognized and promoted. Demonstrate your leadership skills inside and outside the office. You do not need a title to show you have what it takes to become an exceptional leader.

Are you the person at work who blames others and finds fault with managers, your situation, the economy, or society? Do you blame others for not getting promoted? Are you playing the victim, or are you taking personal responsibility for having a good job, relationships, and life? Who are you in this responsibility scenario?

Self-Assessment Questions

Have you ever considered what costs we must cover for a $3 item? The cost to buy the product, and what else? Generate a list of expenses.	
Do you know what food and drink items are most popular? Do you know what items are slower-selling items? Be ready to discuss.	
What additional project would you like to take on and discuss with your kitchen supervisor?	
What skills and knowledge do you want to develop next?	
Do you see opportunities to help a team member who may be overworked? What are they? Be ready to discuss.	
In what area do you want to become an expert?	

Coach/Mentor Questions

Have you ever considered what costs we must cover for a $3 item? The cost to buy the product, and what else? Let's discuss those expenses.	
Do you know what food and drink items are most popular? Do you know what items are slower-selling items? Let's discuss.	
What skills and knowledge do you want to develop next?	
What do you think senior managers value in high-potential employees?	
Do you see opportunities to help a team member who may be overworked?	
In what area do you want to become an expert?	
How can you develop your initiative?	
How can I help you learn more about revenue and responsibility?	
How can I support you?	
Assignment for Next Week:	

S IS FOR SERVE SAFE

> *"Knowing yourself is key to all wisdom."*
> —Aristotle

The National Restaurant Association develops and administers the Serve Safe Food Safety Training and Certification Program. Everyone who works in food service must have the food service handler's certification. Think of it this way: When you are in hospitality, there are certain standards you must follow, such as hand hygiene. This is also true in the food service industry. While they are similar, they are also different, and we must adhere to both. This week is to refresh your memory of some of the questions posed in the practice exams. You can Google "Serve Safe" to access all five practice exams. Here is the link to the website: https://www.servsafe.com/ or see sample questions in the mentee section of this article.

The exam is enhanced each year as our industry changes. It addresses providing safe food, forms of contamination, safe food handling techniques, purchasing, receiving, storage, ensuring safe facilities, pest management, cleaning, and sanitizing.

If you have taken the exam, how have your food service preparations changed?

Self-Assessment Questions

How has your food service preparation changed at home and work?	
Let's Review: One of the FDA-recommended food safety responsibilities of a manager is: __A. Making and approving staff schedules __B. Providing maintenance for the facility __C. Supervising food handlers to ensure hot and cold food holding temperatures are regularly monitored __D. Inspecting the quality of food items prepared off-premises for serving in the facility	
How can food handlers reduce or increase the risk of food contamination? __A. Washing their hands after using the restroom __B. Taking medication after visiting a sick friend __C. Storing cleaning products in an easy-to-reach location in the kitchen __D. Rinsing knives and cutting boards with hot water when moving between prep items	

How long should you scrub your hands and arms during handwashing? __A. Five to ten seconds __B. Ten to fifteen seconds __C. Fifteen to twenty seconds __D. Twenty to twenty-five seconds	
You should never handle ready-to-eat food with bare hands in what situation? __A. You should never handle ready-to-eat foods with bare hands, regardless of the situation __B. When there is not a proper handwashing station available __C. When serving food to a high-risk population, like children or the elderly __D. When the food is cooked to at least 140 degrees F	
When should a delivery be inspected? __A. After placing all products in their appropriate storage areas __B. When staff has time to inspect the delivery correctly __C. Immediately upon receiving the delivery __D. When the specific staff responsible for inspecting deliveries is available	

Why is it advisable to only remove the amount of food you can prep in a brief period from the cooler?

__A. To prevent time-temp abuse

__B. To prevent cross-contamination

__C. To prevent excess food waste

__D. To reduce clutter and mess on food prep surfaces

If you discover that a steam table holding hot soup has broken down and the soup may have been unheated for as long as three hours, what should you do with the soup?

__A. Reheat the soup to 135 degrees F and transfer it to a working steam table

__B. Fix the steam table and reheat the soup

__C. Discard the soup, heat a new batch to 135 degrees F, and place it in a working steamtable

__D. Combine the cooled soup with new, properly heat the soup, and place it in a working steamtable

For what can handwashing sinks be used?

__A. Handwashing only

__B. Rinsing fresh produce

__C. Thawing frozen product

__D. Rinsing bar towels and sanitizer towels

Performing procedural checks every shift to identify problems and comparing and analyzing temperature logs each week are examples of which principle in the HAACP system?

__A. Principle 5: Identifying corrective actions

__B. Principle 6: Verifying that the system works

__C. Principle 4: Establishing monitoring procedures

__D. Principle 7: Establishing procedures for record-keeping and documentation

What did you learn from this exercise?

Coach/Mentor Questions

How has your food service preparation changed at home and work?	
Let's Review: One of the FDA-recommended food safety responsibilities of a manager is: __A. Making and approving staff schedules __B. Providing maintenance for the facility __C. Supervising food handlers to ensure hot and cold food holding temperatures are regularly monitored __D. Inspecting the quality of food items prepared off-premises for serving in the facility	
How can food handlers reduce or increase the risk of food contamination? __A. Washing their hands after using the restroom __B. Taking medication after visiting a sick friend __C. Storing cleaning products in an easy-to-reach location in the kitchen __D. Rinsing knives and cutting boards with hot water when moving between prep items	
How long should you scrub your hands and arms during handwashing? __A. Five to ten seconds __B. Ten to fifteen seconds __C. Fifteen to twenty seconds __D. Twenty to twenty-five seconds	
You should never handle ready-to-eat food with bare hands in what situation? __A. You should never handle ready-to-eat foods with bare hands, regardless of the situation __B. When there is not a proper handwashing station available __C. When serving food to a high-risk population, like children or the elderly __D. When the food is cooked to at least 140 degrees F	

When should a delivery be inspected? __A. After placing all products in their appropriate storage areas __B. When staff has time to inspect the delivery correctly __C. Immediately upon receiving the delivery __D. When the specific staff responsible for inspecting deliveries is available	
Why is it advisable to only remove the amount of food you can prep in a brief period from the cooler? __A. To prevent time-temp abuse __B. To prevent cross-contamination __C. To prevent excess food waste __D. To reduce clutter and mess on food prep surfaces	
If you discover that a steam table holding hot soup has broken down and the soup may have been unheated for as long as three hours, what should you do with the soup? __A. Reheat the soup to 135 degrees F and transfer it to a working steam table __B. Fix the steam table and reheat the soup __C. Discard the soup, heat a new batch to 135 degrees F, and place it in a working steamtable __D. Combine the cooled soup with new, properly heat the soup, and place it in a working steamtable	
For what can handwashing sinks be used? __A. Handwashing only __B. Rinsing fresh produce __C. Thawing frozen product __D. Rinsing bar towels and sanitizer towels	

Performing procedural checks every shift to identify problems and comparing and analyzing temperature logs each week are examples of which principle in the HAACP system? __A. Principle 5: Identifying corrective actions __B. Principle 6: Verifying that the system works __C. Principle 4: Establishing monitoring procedures __D. Principle 7: Establishing procedures for record-keeping and documentation	
What did you learn from this Serve Safe exercise?	
How can I support you?	
Assignment for Next Week:	

T IS FOR TEAMWORK

> *"Make it a habit of telling people thank you—to express
> your appreciation sincerely without expecting anything in
> return. Truly appreciate those around you, and you will soon
> find many others around you. Truly appreciate life,
> and honestly, you will find you have more of it."*
> –Ralph Marston

In the bustling environment of a prison kitchen, teamwork is not just a desirable trait; it is an essential component for success. The kitchen is a place where every individual's effort contributes to the overall outcome, and the importance of working together cannot be overstated.

Teamwork in the kitchen begins with understanding that each role, no matter how small it may seem, is crucial. From the person chopping vegetables to the one washing dishes, every task is interconnected. When everyone performs their duties efficiently and supports one another, the kitchen operates like a well-oiled machine. This synergy ensures that meals are prepared on time, dietary needs are met, and food safety standards are upheld.

Effective communication is the backbone of teamwork. In a prison kitchen, clear and concise communication helps prevent misunderstandings and errors. It is important to keep each other informed about the status of tasks, any issues that arise, and any changes in the menu or schedule. Regular meetings and briefings can help ensure that everyone agrees and working towards the same goals.

Trust and respect are fundamental to building a strong team. Trusting your colleagues to perform their tasks correctly and efficiently allows you to focus on your own responsibilities. Respecting each other's contributions fosters a positive work environment where everyone feels valued. This mutual respect and trust can lead to increased job satisfaction and a more cohesive team.

In a dynamic environment like a prison kitchen, problems can arise unexpectedly. Whether it's a shortage of ingredients or a malfunctioning piece of equipment, the ability to solve problems quickly and adapt to changing circumstances is crucial. Teamwork enables the pooling of ideas and resources to find practical solutions. When everyone works together to overcome challenges, it resolves the issue at hand and strengthens the team's bond.

Teamwork also provides opportunities for learning and development. By working closely with others, you can learn new skills, techniques, and approaches to tasks. Sharing knowledge and experiences helps everyone to improve and grow. Encouraging a continuous learning and support culture can lead to a more skilled and versatile team.

A positive work environment is essential for maintaining morale and productivity. Teamwork fosters a sense of camaraderie and belonging. When team members support and encourage each other, it creates a more enjoyable and motivating atmosphere. Celebrating successes, no matter how small, and recognizing each other's efforts, can boost morale and reinforce the importance of teamwork. This is important to remember inside and out of prison. One day you may be the manager, and will need to know how to lead and encourage teamwork.

In conclusion, teamwork is the cornerstone of a successful prison kitchen. It ensures that tasks are completed efficiently, problems are solved effectively, and a positive work environment is maintained. By valuing each other's contributions, communicating clearly, and supporting one another, kitchen employees can work together to achieve their common goals. Remember, in the kitchen, we are stronger together.

Self-Assessment Questions

How do you currently communicate with your team members during your shift? Are there ways to improve this communication?	
Can you recall a time when teamwork helped solve a problem in the kitchen? What did you learn from that experience?	
What steps can you take to build trust and respect among your colleagues?	
How do you handle conflicts or disagreements with team members? What strategies can you use to resolve them constructively?	
In what ways can you contribute to creating a positive and supportive work environment in the kitchen?	
What skills or knowledge can you share with your team to help them improve?	
How do you adapt to changes or unexpected challenges in the kitchen? How can teamwork help in these situations? How can you encourage continuous learning and development within your team?	
What are some ways you can recognize and celebrate the efforts and successes of your team members?	
What actions can you take to ensure that everyone feels valued and included in the team?	

Coach/Mentor Questions

How do you currently communicate with your team members during your shift? Are there ways to improve this communication?	
Can you recall a time when teamwork helped solve a problem in the kitchen? What did you learn from that experience?	
What steps can you take to build trust and respect among your colleagues?	
How do you handle conflicts or disagreements with team members? What strategies can you use to resolve them constructively?	
In what ways can you contribute to creating a positive and supportive work environment in the kitchen?	
What skills or knowledge can you share with your team to help them improve?	
How do you adapt to changes or unexpected challenges in the kitchen? How can teamwork help in these situations? How can you encourage continuous learning and development within your team?	
What are some ways you can recognize and celebrate the efforts and successes of your team members?	
What actions can you take to ensure that everyone feels valued and included in the team?	
How can I support you?	
Assignment for Next Week:	

 U IS FOR UNIQUE

> *"A human being is a single being.*
> *Unique and unrepeatable."*
> —Eileen Caddy

You are unique and talented, so try not to compare yourself to others. This is true at work, at play, and in life. I enjoy taking yoga classes. I love the way it makes me feel. The teachers are always reminding us not to compare our practice to others. Every person comes to yoga each day. Some days, the postures are natural. Some days, the poses are more challenging. Regardless, I am mindful of my self-talk. It is always positive. I made a point of going to yoga and giving myself the gift of an hour. I do not look around and compare myself to new practitioners or experienced practitioners. I see the beauty in each person. After all, it is my practice.

This is also true at work; your uniqueness is expressed through authenticity. You are real, genuine, and one of a kind. Positively capitalize on your uniqueness. Be engaging, fresh, current, and relevant. Being unique is not being or feeling superior. The YogaOne Studio owner and author of the *Love Revolution*, Roger Rippy, shared his story about this. He said, "You have to run your own race." He added, "The question is how you acknowledge, appreciate, and develop what your uniqueness is and what you have."

- How are you unique?
- What do you love doing?
- What do you enjoy?
- How can you serve others?
- What inspires you?

Be willing to share information and help others no matter what their age. Reinforce the idea that the company made a good decision hiring you.

Self-Assessment Questions

How are you unique?	
What do you love doing?	
What do you enjoy?	
How can you serve others?	
What inspires you?	

Coach/Mentor Questions

Every person is unique. Where are you exceptional? How does that serve you?	
What do you love doing?	
Whom does it serve?	
How can you share this with others?	
What do you enjoy? How can you share with others to better serve them?	
What inspires you? How can you use your inspiration to serve others?	
What have you always wanted to do? How can that serve others?	
How can I support you?	
Assignment for Next Week:	

 V IS FOR VISION

> *"The visionary starts with a clean sheet of paper and reimagines the world."*
> —Malcolm Gladwell

What vision do you have for your life? Visualize what you want for yourself. What do you love doing? What type of career do you want? What job roles? What salary do you want to earn? What do you want regarding financial security? What educational level do you want to attain? Where do you want to live? What do you want your relationships to look like? What hobbies do you enjoy? What about spirituality?

Who do you see yourself becoming? How does it feel? What do you see? Take a mental picture. Write it down. Create a vision board that inspires and motivates you and brings you joy. Place it where you'll see it every day. There is scientific evidence to support the power of visualization. What you focus on, you achieve.

What are people saying about you? The more you can bring all your senses into this vision you have for yourself, the more likely you will achieve it. Write it down. Look at it every day. Repeat it as an affirmation. Write the goals you want to achieve. Do you believe it is possible? Great, if yes. Get out of your own way and make it happen. You are more likely to achieve the life you want if you write your goals down and revisit them daily.

As an emerging leader, you must envision where you want to take your organization, department, or team. The more you can paint the picture for them, the more likely you will achieve it. When you are storytelling about the vision, bring in all senses.

One of my former bosses asked us to engage in this great exercise. He would describe the project we were working on in detail. He then asked us to close our eyes and think about three years from now. He would say, "Let's pretend we are at a company picnic celebrating our success. What would we have accomplished? What were people saying about the organization internally and externally? How did you feel? What was the day like? What sounds could you hear? What did you see around you?" By the time we finished the exercise, everyone could see in their mind's eye where we were going and how we would feel when we got there. It is truly inspiring! At subsequent meetings, he would remind us of the picnic picture so we would not lose sight of where we were going and what we could accomplish.

Good luck!

Self-Assessment Questions

What do you want for yourself and your life?	
What type of career do you want? What job roles? What salary do you want to earn?	
What do you want in terms of financial security?	
What educational level do you want to attain?	
Where do you want to live?	
What do you want your relationships to look like?	
What hobbies do you enjoy?	
What about spirituality?	
Who do you see yourself becoming? How does it feel? What do you see? Write it down Create a vision board that inspires and motivates you and brings you joy. Place it somewhere you'll see it every day.	

Coach/Mentor Questions

As an emerging leader, you must have a vision of where you want to take your organization, department, or team. How would you describe that picture?	
What is the story?	
If you were the leader, could you lead the picnic exercise as described? How would you bring in all the senses? Share your version of this exercise with me.	
How can I support you?	
Assignment for Next Week:	

> *"If you tell the truth, you don't have to remember anything."*
> —Mark Twain

I am often surprised at how people tell trivial lies. They feel justified for whatever reason. Example: "I am going to take home office supplies. It's no big deal. The company can afford it." Would you feel the same way if you owned the company?

Years ago, I took over a company in desperate financial trouble. I was uncertain for a time whether we would meet payroll every other week. I needed the employees to understand the situation without causing panic. So, I had a little fun with it and asked them to all return our special signature pens the next day. I called it "Amnesty Day." I was looking for a thousand ways to reduce expenses without losing sight of all the details. The next day, we had over a thousand custom signature pens returned. Have I made my point?

It seemed like no big deal for the employees, but it was a symbol for all of us to work together and turn the situation around, and we did. You might feel someone mistreated you; you deserve something and justify it. A white lie is a *lie*. Webster defines a lie as making an untrue statement intending to deceive. Over time, people forget what the truth is. Lying has a way of holding you hostage. You can justify all you want, but it costs you. It costs you integrity, relationships, jobs, freedom, and authenticity.

A second example is when you tell your supervisor the report is done, but it isn't. You built time to turn it in on time, but you lied to your boss about the report's present state.

Another example is social media. How truthful are you in presenting yourself on social media? Your photo? Your resume? Your relationships? Your reputation? Are these truthful or lies?

Other examples in food service and nutrition include stealing time, not communicating or taking responsibility, and not following a recipe or portion control. What other examples can you think of?

Be careful: Big Brother is always watching.

Self-Assessment Questions

What white lies have you told?	
How did you justify them?	
What did it cost you? Or what could it cost you?	
Do you ever think white lies become more significant over time?	

Coach/Mentor Questions

What did you think about "Amnesty Day" and the returned pens?	
Do you think most people feel justified in telling white lies? What do you think the point of it is?	
Do you think there is ever a time when a white lie is justified?	
How can you create a culture of truth and integrity as a future leader?	
How do you model transparency?	
How can I support you?	
Assignment for Next Week:	

> *"The X-Factor saved me."*
> —James Arthur

Exceptional leaders have the X-Factor. These traits of exceptional leaders are distinct from general leadership traits. Most people cannot describe the traits of an exceptional leader as they have not had the experience of working for one. Based on my experience, I created these traits that exist in *exceptional* leaders:

- Authentic: Genuine, transparent, and comfortable with who they are
- Depth: Understand the organization and themselves across all boundaries, willing to try new things and take risks
- Eclectic: Come to the position with a varied background of experiences, unique
- Energy of Being: Have the required energy level in good times and bad, resilient
- Generosity of Spirit: The ability to connect and relate to human beings, heart-centered, culturally sensitive
- Texture: Bring a sense of creativity when approaching each situation, multi-dimensional
- Visionary: Able to plan and inspire others to achieve the vision, mission, and goals

So, what is your X-Factor? What is your unique talent? How can you positively affect the outcome of the organization in your role?

Can you relate to any of the exceptional leadership traits? Are you authentic, creative, or eclectic? Do you have depth? Do you have a variety of experiences? Do you have a presence? Do you have texture? Do you have credibility? Are you innovative? Do you have a generosity of spirit? Are you interesting? Are you a visionary? How many of these talents do you possess? Given your assessment, would you want to promote yourself? Tell the truth.

Self-Assessment Questions

What is your X-Factor?	
What is your unique talent?	
How can you positively affect the outcome of the organization in your role?	
Can you relate to any of the seven exceptional leadership traits? a. Authentic b. Depth c. Eclectic d. Energy of Being e. Generosity of Spirit f. Texture g. Visionary	
How many of these talents do you possess?	
Given your assessment, would you want me to promote you?	

Coach/Mentor Questions

Let's discuss each of these seven traits of an exceptional leader. What does it mean to be authentic?	
What does it mean to have depth?	
What does it mean to be eclectic? What experiences do you bring?	
What is your energy level? How resilient are you in tough times? Give me an example.	
Do you feel you have a generosity of spirit? Do you think you can connect and relate to other people?	
Do you have texture? Do you bring a sense of creativity when approaching each situation? Give me an example.	
Do you feel that one day, you will have the ability to be a visionary? Can you inspire others to achieve the vision, mission, and goals? Give me an example.	
How can I support you?	
Assignment for Next Week:	

Y IS FOR YEARNING

> *"There are three ingredients for a good life:*
> *learning, earning, and yearning."*
> —Christopher Morley

Do you have an innate yearning to become a better you? Do you have a zest for life? Do you have a love for learning? Do you yearn to live a different kind of life? Do you yearn to travel and experience new things? This is not to say you are unsatisfied, but you have energy that encompasses the essence of your being. Yearning is not related to age. Yearning can exist at any age.

Yearning is a strong desire for something.

I yearned to teach at the college level, share my professional experiences, and mentor others professionally, distinct from coaching. I had academic credentials. I had business experience and a proven track record, but I did not have the tools to deliver an engaging classroom experience at the beginning of my new career. The yearning was incredible, yet I knew I had to go to work and learn as much as possible to master the art and science of teaching. I credit that yearning for carrying me through those tough times so I could obtain personal and professional mastery. I believe all things are possible with yearning, effort, and persistence.

So, explore your possibilities. Explore your values. Explore your beliefs.

What do you yearn for in your life? Be specific and go for it!

Self-Assessment Questions

For what do you yearn?	
How can you start to make this happen?	
What could stop you?	
What is your timeline?	
How will you measure your success?	

Coach/Mentor Questions

For what do you yearn?	
How can you start to make this happen?	
What could stop you?	
What is your timeline?	
How will you measure your success?	
How can I support you?	
Assignment for Next Week:	

Z IS FOR ZONE

> *""Everything is energy, and that's all there is to it. Match the frequency of the reality you want, and you can't help but get that reality. It can be no other way. This is not philosophy. This is physics. "*
> —Albert Einstein

I have often heard athletes describe being in the zone—when everything they do seems to go in the right direction. I'm sure you have your favorite stories and examples, so you can imagine what being in the zone feels like.

Being in the zone is described as being in the flow, flow state, or in a groove. Have you ever lost track of time because you were in the flow or the zone? Now that we have come to trait Z, number twenty-six, do you feel you are in the zone? Have you ever been in the zone? What does it feel like? What were you doing? Describe the sensations. How can you get back there if you are not in the zone now? What is your energy level? What goals have you set, or what actions are you taking?

Sarah Chang wrote a great article on "The Best Tricks for Getting in the Zone at Work." She describes tools to get back in the flow state. Getting back in the zone or achieving a state of flow can significantly enhance your productivity and performance. Here are some effective tricks to help you get back in the zone:

1. Set Clear Goals:

   o Define what you want to achieve before you start working. Clear, specific goals provide direction and motivation, making it easier to focus.

2. Eliminate Distractions:

   o Create a distraction-free environment. Turn off notifications, close unnecessary tabs, and find a quiet space to work.

3. Find Your Optimal Time:

   o Identify the time of day when you are most productive and schedule your most important tasks during this period.

4. Break Tasks into Smaller Steps:

   o Breaking tasks into manageable steps can make them less overwhelming and help you maintain focus.

5. Use a Timer:

   o Techniques like the Pomodoro Technique, where you work for twenty-five minutes and then take a five-minute break, can help maintain concentration and prevent burnout.

6. Listen to Music:

   o Some people find that listening to music, especially instrumental or ambient music, can help them focus and get into the zone.

7. Stay Hydrated and Eat Healthily:

   o Drink enough water and eat healthy snacks to keep your energy levels up. Avoid sugary drinks and junk food that can lead to energy crashes.

8. Take Regular Breaks:

   o Short breaks can help refresh your mind and prevent fatigue. Use these breaks to stretch, walk around, or do something relaxing.

9. Practice Mindfulness and Meditation:

   o Mindfulness and meditation can help clear your mind and improve your ability to focus. Even a few minutes of deep breathing can make a difference.

10. Create a Routine:

   o Establishing a consistent routine can signal to your brain that it's time to focus, making it easier to get in the zone.

By incorporating these strategies into your daily routine, you can improve your ability to get back in the zone and maintain high levels of productivity and performance.

What project can you work on that challenges you? What goals do you want to accomplish? Can you create a space with little or no interruptions?

What are you not doing that you need to be doing? What should you keep doing that works or stop doing? Are you committed to getting back to being in the zone state and taking it to the next level? Turn off the TV and get started!

Self-Assessment Questions

Are you in the zone?	
Describe a time when you were in the zone and how it felt.	
Do you feel you are in the zone now?	
How can you get back in the zone?	
Read the article by Sarah Chang and check out the resources.	
Final Reflection: Write what you have accomplished over the last twenty-six weeks. Be ready to discuss.	
What's next?	

Coach/Mentor Questions

Are you in the zone?	
After reading the article by Sarah Chang, what do you think?	
How can you help your team get in the zone?	
Final Reflection: Now that you have completed twenty-six weeks, what have you accomplished? Use the self-awareness inventory again to evaluate your progress.	
What have you learned?	
How have you changed?	
What's next?	
How can I support you?	
Assignment for Next Week:	

Post Self-Assessment Inventory

	Rate yourself one to ten, one being poor and ten being excellent	Plan to improve/resources utilized
Attitude		
Brand		
Communication		
Diversity and Drive Performance		
Energy		
Foodservice		
Gratitude		
Hospitality		
Integrity		
Jaded		
Knowledgeable		
Lifelong Learner		
Mindset		
Nutrition		
Opportunity		
Problem Solver		
Question		
Revenue and Responsibility		
Serve Safe		
Teamwork		
Unique		
Vision		
White Lies		
X-Factor		
Yearning		
Zone		

DEVELOPING A REENTRY PLAN

Without a plan for reentry, it is quite possible you will see no other option other than going back to illegal activities. You need to prepare for access to food, transportation, clothing, shelter, personal identification documents, and much more. Working with your mentor, you can develop a plan for post-release.

According to the Urban Institute Justice Policy Center in Washington, DC, you need to plan for needs, and here are their recommendations (2008):

- *Transportation*: Find out if the prison provides transportation upon release or if you must make arrangements.
- *Clothing, food amenities*: You will have clothes to leave the prison and hopefully basic toiletries. You will need a list of information about accessing food resources.
- *Financial resources*: You will receive a nominal amount of money at release time. In Texas, it's $100 unless you are on parole; you receive an additional $100 when you meet with your parole officer for the first time. Every state varies, so find out.
- *Documentation*: You will need to obtain a state-issued identification card.
- *Housing*: You will need to decide where to stay post-release. The prison might be able to provide a list of resources and where beds are available. If you are considering returning to your hometown, make sure it is not the place that created the environment for the crime. If you go back to that place, you certainly will be going back to prison sooner rather than later.
- *Employment and education*: Ensure you have the appropriate forms and referrals for the process of finding and keeping a job. Make sure you have copies of any completion certificate of education, training, or certifications you participated in.
- *Health care*: Depending on your mental and physical well-being, have a list of programs and contact information you can access post-release.
- *Support systems*: Make sure you obtain a handbook of community resources. Contact family or friends and notify them of your release date and plan.

Each person released from prison will have their own unique set of circumstances based on the crime. Another distinction is how an inmate is released, whether it is a supervised release or unsupervised release.

Finally, women who get caught up in the criminal justice system and have extensive histories of drug abuse are likely to be clinically depressed, have low self-esteem, have fewer job skills than their male counterparts, tend to be homeless, and have problems with intimate partners (Lavigne et al. 2008, 30). For women working with mentors, develop a post-release plan focused on employment readiness, housing, and family reunification.

The final steps in developing your release plan include asking these questions: What do you need? What do you have?

CHECKLIST FOR INTEGRATION

Item	Completed: Place an X in the row.	Need to Obtain: Place an X in the row.	Plan/Timeline
☐ Social Security number			
☐ State ID			
☐ Birth certificate			
☐ Copy of release stipulations/rules			
☐ Driver's license			
☐ Transportation determined: family members, friends, or public transportation—cost, routes, etc.			
☐ Housing located: family, friends, halfway house, shelter—cost			
☐ Mailing address/receiving documents/organizational folder			

☐ Library card (libraries provide internet access)			
☐ Email address			
☐ Phone/internet			
☐ Educational credentials/ transcript requests			
☐ Résumé			
☐ Personal incarceration statement			
☐ Professional clothing: Dress for Success, Goodwill, or your church may be able to help			
☐ Employment: job or signed employment release			
☐ Access to food: food pantry/shelter			
☐ Budget			
☐ Support groups (e.g., VA, PTSD, NAMI)			
☐ Substance abuse support (NA, AA, etc.)			
☐ Spiritual/church home			

☐ Counseling support			
☐ Health care			
☐ Healthy parenting classes			
☐ Healthy recreational opportunities			
☐ Exercise			
☐ Voting impact of your crime			
☐ Check-ins with parole/probation officer			
☐ Nearest bank/bank account			
☐ Reconnecting with family and children			
☐ Changes in society since incarceration			
☐ Warrant clearance cleanup/ criminal record check			
☐ Daily schedule and routines to follow			
☐ Court dates/debts			
☐ Knowing the legal consequences of your conviction			

☐ Trusted advisor/mentor post-release			
☐ Maintaining the daily questions to improve behavior and choices			
☐ List of resources available in your hometown			

For veterans, the local VA hospital provides various services and programs to support you.

CAREER DEVELOPMENT TOOLS

One effective way to get started is to fill out a job application so you know what information you need before creating a résumé. You can complete this and take it when filling out a real job application.

Transforming the Past into a Future: Writing Exercise

Complete the following:

Before we get started, think about your transferable skills.

1. What skills did you have before incarceration (legal or illegal)?
2. How can the illegal skills be transformed into something positive and provide a career for you?
3. What skills have you gained while in prison?
4. What skills can you share with an employer during an interview?

Employment Application (For Inmate Mentee)

Company Name

Applicant Information

Full Name: _____   Date: _____

      Last   First   Middle .

Address: _____

      Street Address   Apartment/Unit #

_____

      City   State   ZIP Code

Phone: _____ Email _____

Date
Available: _____   *Social
Security No.:* _____   *Desired
Salary:* $ _____

Position
Applied for: _____

Are you a citizen of the United
States?   YES   NO   *If no, are you authorized to work in
                                 ☐   ☐   the US?*   YES   NO
                                                                                  ☐   ☐

Have you ever worked for this
company?   YES   NO   *If yes, when?* _____
                                 ☐   ☐

Have you ever been convicted
of a felony?   YES   NO
                                 ☐   ☐

If yes, explain: _____

Education

High School: _____   Address: _____

From: _____ – _____   *Did you
                              graduate?* YES   NO   Diploma:
                                          ☐   ☐   _____

College: _____   Address: _____

From: _____ – _____   *Did you
                              graduate?* YES   NO   Degree:
                                          ☐   ☐   _____

Other: _____   Address: _____

From: _____ – _____   *Did you
                              graduate?* YES   NO   Degree:
                                          ☐   ☐   _____

References

Please list three professional references.

Full Name: _____   *Relationship:* _____

Company: _____   *Phone:* _____

Address: _____

Full Name: _____   *Relationship:* _____

Company: _____   *Phone:* _____

Address: _____

Full Name: _____   *Relationship:* _____

Company: _____   *Phone:* _____

Address: _____

Previous Employment (Begin with most recent employment)

Company: _____   *Phone:*_____

Address: _____   *Supervisor:*_____

Job Title: _____ *Starting Salary:* **$**_____ *Ending Salary:* **$**_____

Responsibilities: _____

From: _____ – _____ *Reason for Leaving:* _____

May we contact your previous supervisor for
a reference?   YES   NO
                                ☐   ☐

_____

_____

Company: _____   *Phone:*_____

Address: _____   *Supervisor:*_____

Job Title: _____ *Starting Salary:* **$**_____ *Ending Salary:* **$**_____

Responsibilities: _____

From: _____ – _____ *Reason for Leaving:* _____

May we contact your previous supervisor for a reference?

YES ☐ NO ☐

_____

_____

Company: _____ Phone:_____

Address: _____ Supervisor:_____

Job Title: _____ Starting Salary: **$**_____ Ending Salary: **$**_____

Responsibilities: _____

From: _____ – _____ Reason for Leaving: _____

May we contact your previous supervisor for a reference?

YES ☐ NO ☐

Military Service

Branch: _____ From: _____ To: _____

Rank at Discharge: _____ Type of Discharge: _____

If other than honorable, explain: _____

Disclaimer and Signature

I certify that my answers are true and complete to the best of my knowledge.
If this application leads to employment, I understand that false or misleading information in my application or interview may result in my release.

Signature: _____ Date: _____

Creating A Résumé

These are activity worksheets that will help you get started creating a résumé.

Functional Résumé

For adults in transition, the recommended format for creating a résumé is the functional résumé. In a functional résumé, you do not list the years of employment, which will allow you some flexibility, and you later explain any gaps in the interview. To prepare for this, think about jobs you might like to apply for. List them below.

What is your job objective?

My job objective is:

_____

What skills are needed for this job?

What education is needed for this job?

What experience is needed for this job?

What skills and abilities do you have for this job? Where are the gaps?

Now, let's discover all the things you have accomplished in your life so far:

- What problems have you solved?

- What responsibilities have you taken on?

- Have you been promoted in prison or received a certificate?

- What difference have you made, and why does it matter?

Describe some of your achievements. Use action verbs (manage, communicate, research, design, teach, help, etc.).

Now, list your work history:

Work History

Title of the Job (List most recent first)	Duties	City, State
Title of the Job	Duties	City, State
Title of the Job	Duties	City, State

Education and Training

List your education, training, and certifications.

Education	Training	Certifications

What was the name of the degree, school, and school location (city, state)?

Summary Statement of Key Points

List some of the soft skills you possess, such as excellent communication, outstanding customer service, adaptability, being a team player, and being punctual.

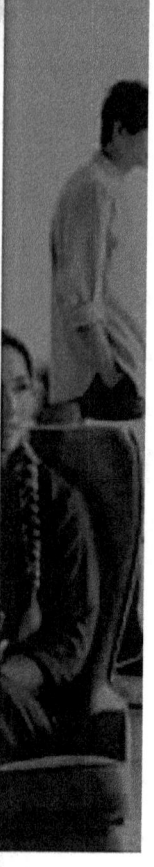

KATHLEEN JONES

CONTACT

example@example.com

555-555-5555

123 Main Street,
San Francisco, CA 94122

EDUCATION

2009

**Bachelor of Arts - Early
Childhood Educatio**

San Francisco, CA

SKILLS

- Personnel records maintenance
- New hire orientation
- Administrative skills
- Compensation/payroll
- Hiring and retention
- Benefits administrator
- HRIS applications proficient
- Policies implementation

PROFESSIONAL SUMMARY

Experienced HR professional with a bachelor's degree in Early Childhood Education and a passion for working with children and their families. Organized, personable, and action-oriented with a strong ability to communicate efficiently.

WORK EXPERIENCE

HR/Accouting Assistant
Dancer Solutions | San Francisco, CA

11/2004 - 10/2011
- Client facing interaction with leading Central Ohio business including Bath and Body Works, Coach, Lane Bryant, Value City Furniture, and Victoria's Secret.
- Supported accounting functions, including accounts payable and receivable.
- Developed and implemented company HR procedures that included: the employee handbook, employee benefits, disciplinary measures, and performance reviews.
- Organized company events with multiple vendors for 100+ guests.
- Managed executive calendars and travel.
- Developed onboarding protocols and trained new company employees.

HR Assistant
Macy's | San Francisco, CA

05/2002 - 11/2004
- Promoted from part-time seasonal employee to full-time within 6 months.
- Responsible for screening and job placement for applicants.
- Implemented new employee training courses.
- Supported accounting functions including payroll.
- Organized large company events with multiple vendors for 150+ guests.

Drafting Your Résumé

Now that you've worked through all the parts of a résumé, it is time to begin writing your own.

Sample

Name Email address Phone Number	
Objective:	
Summary of Qualifications	
Relevant Experience	
Work History	
Education/Training Proof of Education/Certifications	

Letters of Recommendation/References (Separate Documents)

Make a list of three professional references and three personal references, if possible. Make sure you ask before listing their names. Keep the list with their complete names, addresses, phone numbers, and email addresses with you.

Professional Reference	Name	Address (City, State, Zip Code)	Email Address	Phone Number
1.				
2.				
3.				
Personal Reference	Name	Address (City, State, Zip Code)	Email Address	Phone Number
4.				
5.				
6.				

Interviewing

Clothing

Illustrate good and poor examples.

Start preparing what you will wear for the interview and what you will wear to work after you're hired. It should be clean, pressed, conservative, and professional. This may be a struggle for you in the beginning. Organizations like Dress for Success or Goodwill can support getting you started. There are also resale shops. If none of those are available, you might borrow something from a friend, but make sure it is clean and fits.

You might be fortunate enough to work for a company that supplies uniforms, but you'll still need clothing for the interview. Make sure you have a good pair of shoes. You will need work boots in some fields, so keep that in mind when planning.

Personal Hygiene

You only get one chance to make a good first impression. Make sure you bathe, use deodorant, get your nails clipped, comb your hair, shave, put on basic makeup for women, and brush and floss your teeth.

Handshake

Practice your handshake before going to an interview. It should be firm but not hand-crushing. For women, it needs to be firm as well and not weak. This is an important step in making a good impression.

Eye Contact

Looking people in the eye when you meet them or during an interview is key to building trust. Do not stare them down, but look at them.

Punctuality

Once you get an appointment for an interview, map out how long it will take to get there, depending on your transportation. Give yourself extra time to make it to the interview. Ideally, arrive fifteen minutes early. People will watch you as soon as you get to the interview, so be very professional.

Interview Preparation

It is now time to prepare for the interview itself. Practice, practice. Be ready to answer the questions clearly and concisely. A typical interviewer might say, "Tell me about yourself." While most people are prepared to talk about their education and skills, behavior-based questions are slightly different. The employer knows that skill sets are transferable. They want to know they are hiring a person with a set of skills that works within their organization.

The Second Chance Center has great resources for interviewing skill development. One of their suggestions is to use "I" statements instead of "you" statements:

I...

- am motivated
- am resourceful
- am a team player
- am even-tempered
- follow through
- am dependable

I have...

- a positive attitude
- a lot of energy
- good problem-solving skills

I like...

- variety
- challenges
- learning

- working independently
- working on a team

Now that you know how to start, let's create a brief statement about you.

Warm-Up Activity

Take a few minutes and write a statement about yourself using this sample as an outline:

> My name is _____. I am a customer service representative with _____ years making people happy. I am a great listener and can assess the customer's needs quickly. I have excellent follow-through. (List your strengths.)
>
> I am working on _____ (education or certification here). I participated in the Bridges to Life program or life-skills training, etc. (Share what programs you have taken advantage of to better yourself. If you are bilingual, mention it here.)

Highlight your most recent accomplishments, and close by talking about your professional goals as they relate to this employer.

Interviewing is a skill that can be developed. You only get one chance to make a good first impression! You are interviewing the moment you arrive at the location. Keep your energy up. Dress professionally. Employers want enthusiastic people who show up on time, get along with others, and can communicate. Employers want to hire you, so close the interview by sharing why you should be hired and telling them you would really like to work with the organization.

Second Chance Center has a list of ten interview questions and how to respond:

1. Tell me about yourself. (This can be a tricky question. Talk about your highlights [two minutes] and past work experiences. Don't take twenty minutes telling your life story.)

2. Why should we hire you? (Make sure to talk about how your strengths match the position—not because you need a job or are desperate. This may be true, but you cannot let it show.)

3. What is your greatest strength? What is your greatest weakness?

4. Why do you want to work here?

5. Tell me how your skills are a match for this job.

6. When you were employed, why did you leave your last job?

7. I noticed a gap in time on your resume/application, tell me how you have spent your time?

8. Describe a difficult work situation and what you did to overcome it.

9. Where do you see yourself in five years?

10. Do you have any questions for me?

According to Jobcast by Indeed (October 2, 2020), here are some sample behavior-based questions. Practice how you might answer:

- Tell me about a time you handled a challenging situation. What happened, and what was the result?
- Tell me about a time you made a mistake. How did you handle it?
- Tell me about how you work under pressure.
- Give me an example of how you set goals.
- Tell me about a time you were angry, how you handled it, and the outcome.
- Share an example of how you have helped motivate another person.
- Often, at the end of the interview, the employers expect you to ask a few questions.

    Typical questions you might ask are as follows:

    o Can you describe a typical day in this position?
    o To whom will I be reporting?
    o What do you like about working here?
    o What do you find challenging about working here?
    o When will you be making your decision, and how will you notify me?

Discussing Criminal History: The Challenging Questions

How do I answer questions about incarceration?

There are many ways to handle this situation. The Second Chance Center recommends five possible approaches. Regardless, write what you want to share. Practice your response! Don't leave your response to chance.

1. When applying for a job, you might want to attach a statement about your criminal background and then have a conversation with the hiring manager about the job you are applying for and how you are qualified.

2. In the interview, when you are asked, "Tell me about yourself," talk about your strengths and how you are a good fit for the job. Add something like, "In addition to these experiences, I would like to take the time to share something more personal with you about myself" (share your prepared statement).

3. Another way to reveal your past is when the employer asks you about your greatest weakness. Give your prepared statement.

4. At the end of the interview, when the employer has asked all their questions, and you've asked yours, say something like, "Before I leave today, there is something I would like you to know." Then, tell the employer your prepared statement.

5. The interview is over; you did a great job, and they extended an offer. This is the time to accept the offer and a chance to disclose your criminal background to the employer. Share with them your prepared statement.

When discussing your criminal background, be honest but soften how it is presented.

Examples:

- I was in possession of a controlled substance.
- I was using my body as a means of earning a living.
- I was in a verbal/physical confrontation, and as a result, someone lost their life.
- I helped someone during a crime that took place.
- I had unauthorized possession of a firearm.
- I used my authority/access to take money/property that did not belong to me.

Are-You-Ready Checklist

- ☐ How is your confidence level? Your mindset? Your energy level?
- ☐ Résumé—take a copy for each person interviewing you.
- ☐ Bring two pens with black ink.
- ☐ Bring some note-taking paper (a spiral notebook is an option).
- ☐ Know in advance how to get to the location. (Give yourself ample time to get there at least fifteen minutes early.)
- ☐ Take your driver's license/ID card and Social Security card.
- ☐ Produce your letters of recommendation (if asked).
- ☐ Produce your list of references (have the complete contact information with you, including name, address, phone number, and email address; include personal as well as professional references).
- ☐ Research the company in advance—go online.
- ☐ Practice interviewing.
- ☐ Be professionally dressed.
- ☐ Go to the interview alone.
- ☐ Turn off your cell phone; do not take beverages or food into the interview. Do not smoke or chew gum.
- ☐ Get a good night's sleep the night before.
- ☐ Have a firm handshake, but not too strong.
- ☐ Maintain eye contact.
- ☐ Remember the interviewer's name and ask if you can have their card when you leave.
- ☐ Take only the essentials and be organized.

Networking

Start listing people you know who can help you find legal employment. These could include family members, friends, parole officers, ministers, and teachers. The job search can be made easier by carefully thinking through your network and communicating to them what you want to accomplish upon release.

LinkedIn: https://www.linkedin.com/

LinkedIn is the best business social media profile presence you can build. You will need an email address, résumé, and professional photo to get started. Over time, you can build out the sections. It is also a great way to enhance your professional network.

Job-Search Leads

There are many excellent job boards or employment websites. Some of the most robust are the following:

Indeed.com (https://www.indeed.com/)
CareerBuilder.com (https://www.careerbuilder.com/)
SimplyHired.com (https://www.simplyhired.com/)

Once you have your résumé, you can upload it to these employment sites to help direct your job search.

Cover Letter

While not every job requires a cover letter, it is very important to customize your cover letter for each job you are applying for. You might say that is a lot of work. It does require a little effort, but it will pay off. You are asking the employer for a job, so think about this: If you spend a few extra minutes customizing your cover letter so they hire you, it is the equivalent of a year's salary. The answer must be yes; it is worth it!

Now Hired, Now What?

Now that you're hired, what does the employer expect? They expect you to show up on time, dressed and ready to go. They expect you to be able to do all the things you stated in the interview. They expect you to get along with your peers at work and with management. They will not tolerate no-shows or latecomers. They will not tolerate cussing or violence in the workplace. All the work has been done in preparation for release, and working on the soft skills will help you with your transition back into the workplace.

THINGS THEY DO NOT TELL YOU ABOUT REINTEGRATION: LIFE SKILLS FOR SUCCESS

No one can totally know your story and what you have been through. It has been a long journey to get to your day of release. You will be filled with a lot of emotions, from excitement to anxiety or depression. This will not be easy. For several years, your life has been regulated from the time you get up to when you go to bed, including every decision about when you eat, when you work, where and when you can walk, when you have free time, etc. The lighting and noise in the units become a way of life.

Walking out of the prison can give you a moment of euphoria. Hopefully, this book has given you a glimpse of things you need to prepare for. You will have responsibilities you have not had in years.

If you were incarcerated due to drugs, how will you resist the temptation when you are free? Get into and stay in a program with a sponsor. It is a day-to-day battle. You may need to go to meetings *every day* for support.

Build a relationship with social workers so your transition can be supported. Find a church. Your transition can go in one of two directions—you choose.

Get involved outside with support groups, educational programs, and a church as soon as possible. Get a sponsor, counselor, or mentor for support and accountability. Counseling and other support services are free of charge through agencies such as Court Services and the Offenders Supervision Agency.

Register with community health-care providers and keep up with all needed medications.

Know your purpose and self-worth. Keep God first in all things. Keep your daily questions present.

SUMMARY

This book is for you, food service operators and leaders. It is designed for you to coach or mentor your staff in weekly one-on-one meetings. It is a guide to assist you in helping your mentees and/or staff members uncover blind spots on their career pathways. It is a tool for becoming more self-aware. It is a framework to help bring you and your employees closer to becoming better connected and sharing expectations. It will not happen overnight. As a food service employee or leader, you can challenge your employees' thinking and achieve more powerful results in less time.

The reality of the workplace today has a dark side. You can become an agent of change to make the workplace better. According to Randall Beck, managing partner, and Dr. Jim Harter, chief scientist at Gallup (2015), the state of the workplace is alarming and has not changed in the last twenty years (p. 1). Yet that is not entirely true. Some great operators go against this negative perception. The good news is that great managers create the right environment for engagement. Think about organizations like Chick-fil-A or Starbucks. How do we achieve such great customer service experiences for customers? They are hiring from the same potential workforce as you are.

According to Beck and Harter, the bad news is that only 30 percent of US employees are engaged, and only 13 percent worldwide (p. 1). The solution is to acquire great talent and develop that talent. You cannot motivate staff, so hire self-motivated employees and challenge and recognize them.

Robert Hogan and Joyce Hogan, workplace assessment experts (2001), stated between 50 and 75 percent of leaders are ineffective (p.133). So, what explains the situation? In large part, these leaders have blind spots. They cannot connect, relate, hire well, coach, and develop people to build a team. They can be seen as micromanagers, negative, and cynical. Many times, this results in organizational failure. McKinsey and Company (May 2000), a global management consulting firm, stated that only 10 percent of middle managers in most firms qualify as real leaders, and 30 to 50 percent of high-potential managers fail. So, given this alarming state of leadership ineffectiveness, what is the solution?

Just as we have described throughout this book, as a leader, you need the *combination* of knowledge, skills, attitude, fit, and traits to build high-performance teams. Could that be you? Can you build a highly effectively functioning team based on these traits?

Gallup also found that about one in ten people possess enough high talent to manage, and another two in ten people exhibit some characteristics of managerial talent if the company invests in coaching and development (Beck & Harter, 2015, p.2).

What is the root cause of the problem? It starts with making the right initial hire. This is where most companies miss the mark. Just because you have an opening, don't rush to fill it. This will cost you. As I stated earlier, I create sayings I live by. In this situation, I say to myself, "Desperation does not become you." The situation may make you feel desperate to fill the position but make sure you hire the best candidate, not just a warm body.

Once hired, you must coach and develop talent. Treat your employees the way you want to be treated. Didn't we learn that lesson in kindergarten? Why is this lesson so hard for some people? Talent exists in organizations.

My career coaching track record is successful due in large part to finding the right candidates, then investing in each of them through weekly coaching sessions and facilitating leadership academies. Each time we had opportunities for promotion, I would think about all the employees in my organization one by one. What skills, traits, knowledge, and attitudes did they possess? What were we looking for? Where would there be a good match? I have successfully used this approach for the past twenty years. I looked across the organization. I have never believed the career ladder is a straight line. I doubt you do, either. Assuming you make the right hires and hold weekly coaching meetings, you must do more to develop your high-potential employees. We created a leadership academy to further develop these individuals in the organization. I am so proud of the hundreds of people I have coached and mentored to achieve the career of their dreams. I love celebrating their success!

The food service culture must be cultivated. The more you invest in people, the higher returns in engagement, job satisfaction, productivity, and achieving performance indicators. If you just chase the metrics, your results will be short-term.

I am committed to your success and changing the future one conversation at a time.

ABOUT THE AUTHOR

Dr. Kim Nugent is an innovation leadership coach, keynote speaker, best-selling author, founder of Kim Nugent Enterprises LLC, and director of talent and organizational development for Harris Health System. She was recently selected for the prestigious Lifetime Achievement Award for 2022 by IAOTP and chosen to be featured in the 2023 Top 50 Fearless Leaders Publication by the International Association of Top Professionals (IAOTP), 2024 Top 25 Global Impact Award, and 2024 5 of the Most Daring Leaders by ExecLens.

Dr. Kim Nugent has exemplary brilliance in higher education, administration, hospitality operations, marketing, leadership coaching, and as a thriving entrepreneur. She has over three decades of professional experience. Dr. Nugent has demonstrated success and advancement in every position she's ever held. Currently, she serves as the founder of Kim Nugent Enterprises LLC and partners with corporations and individuals to maximize their leadership capacity, productivity, and promotability. Dr. Nugent develops customized research-based leadership academies and faculty development programs to improve employee and student engagement.

Dr. Nugent is a sought-after lecturer, speaker, and Amazon best-selling and award-winning author. To date, Dr. Nugent has written and published eleven books: *From Teacher to Leader: Paving Your Path to Education Administration; From Prison to Possibilities: Paving Your Path; Recruit, Retain, and Reimagine Today's Foodservice Workforce; Paving Your Path: What's Next For High School Graduates: A Promotion Protocol Guide To Manifesting Career Success; Paving Your Path: What's Next For High School Graduates Companion Workbook; Promotion Protocol: Unlock the Secrets of Promotability and Career Success; Promotion Protocol: Coaching Conversations Companion Guide; Did I Say Never?: A Stepparent's Emotional Journey with her Special Needs Son; Finding My Forever Family: Finding Love and Acceptance Through Adoption; 52 Weeks to Exceptional Leadership;* and *From Corrections to Careers: Today's Foodservice Workforce."*

For the Train the Trainer program, contact Kim at:
Kim@drnugentspeaks.com or Nugent1234@gmail.com.

REFERENCES

Alton, L. (2016, September 7). *How sleep deprivation affects your day at the office.* https://www.forbes.com/sites/larryalton/2016/09/07/heres-how-sleep-affects-your-day-at-the-office/#3ed1c8e7820b

Anderson. L. & Krathwohl, D. (2001). *Revised Bloom's taxonomy.* https://thesecondprinciple.com/teaching-essentials/beyond-bloom-cognitive-taxonomy-revised/

Attitude. Retrieved October 24, from https://www.google.com/search?q=attitude+definition&oq=attitude+&aqs=chrome.5.69i57j35i39j0l4.5240j1j8&sourceid=chrome&ie=UTF-8

Beausoleil, M. (2020, March 29). *Ten events that defined a generation: Millennial edition.* Retrieved September 16, 2022, from https://beausoleil.medium.com/ten-events-that-defined-a-generation-millennial-edition-9dd5c2806a32

Beck, R. & Harter, J. (2015). *Managers account for 70 percent of the variance in employee engagement.* Retrieved August 6, 2022, from http://news.gallup.com/businessjournal/182792/managers-account-variance-employee-engagement.aspx

Bloom, B. (1956). *Bloom's taxonomy.* http://www.nwlink.com/~donclark/hrd/bloom.html

Bonaparte, J. (2022, September 12). Recruitment ideas post-COVID. [Phone Interview].

Brainy Quotes. (n.d.). https://www.brainyquote.com/

Bungay, G. (2015, July 13). *Remarkable employees: The characteristics of high potentials.* http://performancecritical.com/remarkable-employees-characteristics-high-potentials/

Carman, T. (2022, June 21). *How many restaurants closed from the pandemic: Here's our best estimate.* Retrieved September 3, 2022, from https://www.washingtonpost.com/food/2022/06/21/covid-restaurant-closures/

Carmody. N. J. (2002). *I am thankful.* [Poem]. Retrieved October 1, 2022, from http://www.midnightangel308.com/i_am_thankful_for.htm

Carnegie, D. (2013). *The five essential people skills: How to assert yourself, listen to others, and resolve conflicts.* Retrieved on September 3, 0222 from https://www.youtube.com/watch?v=zvZbeplavY0

Cavoulacos, A. (n.d.). *Ways to take on more responsibility at work.* Retrieved on January 5, 2018, from https://www.themuse.com/advice/5-ways-to-take-on-more-responsibility-at-work

Chang, S. (n.d.). *The best tricks for getting in the zone at work.* Retrieved January 5, 2018, from https://www.themuse.com/advice/the-best-tricks-for-getting-in-the-zone-at-work.

Connell, S. F. (2022, February 14). *The opportunity for diversity in food service at the top.* Retrieved on September 16, 2022, from https://www.forbes.com/sites/

forbescoachescouncil/2022/02/14/the-opportunity-for-diversity-in-food-service-is-at-the-top/?sh=20894c265d8d

Connellan, T. (2002). *Bringing out the best in others!: 3 keys for business leaders, educators, coaches, and parents.* Retrieved on January 5, 2018, from https://www.amazon.com/Bringing-Out-Best-Others-Educators/dp/188516758X/ref=sr_1_1?ie=UTF8&qid=1520700987&sr=8-1&keywords=bringing+out+the+best+in+others

Dale Carnegie. (2018). Retrieved on January 26, 2018, from https://www.dalecarnegie.com/en/franchise-locations

DeFelice, M. (2019). Retrieved on September 16, 2022, from https://www.forbes.com/sites/manondefelice/2019/10/31/what-gen-z-wants-at-work-will-blow-your-mind/?sh=2d23886fb8e7

Dijulius, J. R. III (2003). *Secret service: Hidden systems that produce unforgettable customer service.* Retrieved on January 5, 2018, from https://www.amazon.com/Secret-Service-Systems-Unforgettable-Customer/dp/0814471714/ref=sr_1_3?ie=UTF8&qid=1520797468&sr=8-3&keywords=secret+service+book

Doyle, A. (2002, July 25). *Top cool jobs in the food industry.* Retrieved on September 16, 2022, from https://www.liveabout.com/cool-jobs-food-industry-2064051

Dweck, C. *(2009). Mindset: How we can learn to fulfill our potential.* Retrieved on January 5, 2018, from https://www.amazon.com/Mindset-Psychology-Carol-S-Dweck/dp/0345472322/ref=sr_1_1?ie=UTF8&qid=1518884922&sr=8-1&keywords=mindset+by+carol+dweck

EHS Network. (2022, July 7). *Reduce food allergy reactions.* Retrieved on September 16, 2022, from https://www.cdc.gov/nceh/ehs/ehsnet/plain_language/reduce-food-allergy-reactions.html

Emmons, R. A. (2004). *The psychology of gratitude.* Retrieved on January 5, 2018, https://www.forbes.com/sites/larryalton/2016/09/07/heres-how-sleep-affects-your-day-at-the-office/#3ed1c8e7820b

Ferrazzi, K. & Raz, T. (2005). *Never eat alone and other secrets to success, one relationship at a time.* Crown Publishing: New York.

Gordon, J. (2007). *How to deal with energy vampires.* Retrieved on January 5, 2018, http://www.jongordon.com/positive-tip-energy-vampires

Grammarly. (2018). Retrieved on January 5, 2018, from https://www.grammarly.com

Hogan, R. & Hogan, J. (2001). Assessing leadership: a view of the dark side. *International Journal of Evaluation and Assessment*, pp. 9, 40–51.

Holmes, L. (2017, December). *10 things grateful people do differently.* Retrieved on January 5, 2018, from https://www.huffingtonpost.com/entry/habits-of-grateful-people_us_565352a6e4b0d4093a588538

Indeed, Editorial Team. (2021, October 29). *Top 12 careers in food.* Retrieved on September 16, 2022, from https://www.indeed.com/career-advice/finding-a-job/careers-in-food

Kaiser, H. (n.d.). *What is problem-solving?* Retrieved on January 5, 2018, https://www.mindtools.com/pages/article/newTMC_00.htm

Kaye, B.& Jordan-Evans, S. (2008). *Love 'em or lose 'em: Getting good people to stay.* Berrett- Koehler Publishers: San Francisco.

Kolenda, J. (2022, September 1). Recruitment ideas post-COVID. [Phone Interview].

LinkedIn Learning. (2022, August 31). *Adding value by diversity.* Retrieved on September 16, 2022, from https://www.linkedin.com/learning/adding-value-through-diversity

Liotta, A. (2012). *Unlocking generational codes: Understanding what makes the generations tick and what ticks them off.* Retrieved on January 5, 2018, http://resultance.com/

Mathews, M. (2022, January 1). *16 reasons why people stay in their jobs.* Retrieved on September 16, 2022, from https://beststepever.com/16-reasons-why-people-stay-in-their-jobs/

Maxwell, J. C. (2003). *Attitude 101: What every leader needs to know.* Retrieved on January 5, 2018, https://www.amazon.com/Attitude-101-Every-Leader-Needs/dp/0785263500

McKinsey & Co. (2000, May). *Leadership development: Where is the ROI?* Retrieved on September 17, 2022, from www.hri.eckerrd.edu

Moran, G. (2017). *Ditch these seven bad habits before 2018 starts.* Retrieved on January 5, 2018, https://www.fastcompany.com/40503547/ditch-these-seven-bad-habits-before-2018-starts

NA (2020, September 19). *13 top careers in food & 5 exciting benefits they offer.* Retrieved on September 1, 2022 from https://www.trade-schools.net/articles/careers-in-food

NA (2018, May 3). *HR advice: Behavioral interviewing yields better results.* Retrieved September 16, 2022, from https://www.bizjournals.com/columbus/news/2018/05/03/hr-advice-behavioral-interviewing-yields-better.html

NA National Speakers Association. (2018). Retrieved on January 5, 2018, https://www.nsaspeaker.org/

Peters, T. (2004). *The brand called you.* Retrieved on January 5, 2018, https://www.fastcompany.com/48979/brand-you-survival-kit

Pfau, B. (2016, April 7). *What do millennials really do at work: The same thing the rest of us do.* Retrieved on September 17, 2022, from https://hbr.org/2016/04/what-do-millennials-really-want-at-work

Pulver, C. (2021). *I love it here: How great leaders create organizations their people never want to leave.* Canada: Raincoast Books.

Reynolds, J. (2017, March 1). *20 characteristics of high-potential employees.* Retrieved on January 5, 2018, from https://www.tinypulse.com/blog/20-characteristics-of-high-potential-employees

Rippy, R. (2017). *Love Revolution: A 21-day program to create a life you love.* Retrieved on January 5, 2018, from https://www.facebook.com/events/880164042160109/

Salvaggio, J. (2022, June 22). Recruitment and retention of staff ideas post-COVID. [Phone Interview].

Schmidt, C. (2022). The power of agile recruiting. Lever. Retrieved on September 17, 2022, from https://www.lever.co/resources/ebook/the-power-of-agile-recruiting/

Serve Safe. (2022). National Restaurant Association. Retrieved on September 16, 2022, from https://www.servsafe.com/

Sinek, S. (2011). *Start with why: How great leaders inspire action.* Retrieved on January 5, 2018, https://www.ted.com/talks/simon_sinek_how_great_leaders_inspire_action

Spaeth, K. (2022). Effective recruitment strategies. Gordon Foodservice. Retrieved on September 16, 2022, from https://www.gfs.com/en-us/ideas/effective-recruitment-strategies

TED Talks. (2018). Retrieved on January 5, 2018, from https://www.youtube.com/channel/UCAuUUnT6oDeKwE6v1NGQxug

Toastmasters International (2018). Retrieved on January 5, 2018, from https://www.toastmasters.org/

The Foundation for Critical Thinking. (2018). Retrieved on January 5, 2018, from https://www.criticalthinking.org/

Warhawk, M. S. (2007, December 27). *No excuses.* [Video]. YouTube. https://www.youtube.com/watch?v=obdd31Q9PqA

Yaffe, P. (2011, October). *The 7% rule fact, fiction or misunderstanding.* DOI: 10.1145/2043155.20453156.

www.ingramcontent.com/pod-product-compliance
Lightning Source LLC
Chambersburg PA
CBHW081326120626

46546CB00011B/3242